INSIDE OUT

True stories of transformed lives from
CROOK COUNTY

Published in Beaverton, Oregon, by Good Catch Publishing.
www.goodcatchpublishing.com
V1.1

Printed in the United States of America

Table of Contents

DEDICATION

This book is dedicated to all those whose lives have been turned inside out — who seek change and yearn to believe a new beginning is possible.

ACKNOWLEDGEMENTS

I would like to thank Dusty Flegel for his vision for this book and Brian Carmack for his hard work in making it a reality.

To the people of Eastside, thank you for your boldness and vulnerability in sharing your personal stories.

This book would not have been published without the amazing efforts of our project manager and editor, Hayley Pandolph. Her untiring resolve pushed this project forward and turned it into a stunning victory. Thank you for your great fortitude and diligence. Deep thanks to our incredible editor in chief, Michelle Cuthrell, and executive editor, Jen Genovesi, for all the amazing work they do.

I would also like to thank our invaluable proofreader, Melody Davis, for the focus and energy she puts into perfecting our words. Lastly, I want to extend our gratitude to the creative and very talented Jenny Randle, who designed the beautiful cover for *Inside Out: True Stories of Transformed Lives from Crook County.*

Daren Lindley
President and CEO
Good Catch Publishing

The book you are about to read
is a compilation of authentic life stories.
The facts are true, and the events are real.
These storytellers have dealt with crisis, tragedy, abuse
and neglect and have shared their most private moments,
mess-ups and hang-ups in order for others to learn and
grow from them. In order to protect the identities of those
involved in their pasts, the names and details of some
storytellers have been withheld or changed.

INTRODUCTION

What do you do when life careens out of control? When addiction overtakes you or abuse chains you with fear? Is depression escapable? Will relationships ever be healthy again? Are we destined to dissolve into an abyss of sorrow? Or will the sunlight of happiness ever return?

Your life really can change. It is possible to become a new person. The seven stories you are about to read prove positively that people right here in our town have stopped dying and started living. Whether you've been beaten by abuse, broken promises, shattered dreams or suffocating addictions, the resounding answer is, "Yes! You can become a new person." The potential to break free from gloom and into a bright future awaits.

Expect inspiration, hope and transformation! As you walk with these real people from our very own city through the pages of this book, you will not only find riveting accounts of their hardships, you will learn the secrets that brought about their breakthroughs. These people are no longer living in the shadows of yesterday; they are thriving with a sense of mission and purpose TODAY. May these stories inspire you to do the same.

PERFECT MATCH
The Story of Dan
Written by Marty Minchin

I lowered myself into the shallow end of the apartment complex pool. The water was cool and made me more buoyant, a welcome relief from carrying around the 60 extra pounds I'd gained since getting married a few months before.

John, my brother, jumped in with me, and I made my way along the wall to the deep end.

I pushed off and eased out into the water toward the other side.

"I've got to get back to the gym and start working out again." I tried to make light of my ballooning body.

The water rushed over my face and into my ears as I circled my arms frantically to breaststroke my way across the width of the pool. I pushed my face out of the water and sucked at the air, but it seemed like my lungs had no room for extra breaths. Kicking and flailing, I barely had enough strength to propel myself 20 feet to the other side.

Mercifully, my hand finally touched the edge of the pool. I lay my head on the side and wondered what had happened to me. I was barely out of high school, and I'd been in shape most of my life.

John floated over and slapped me on the back.

"Dan, if this is what marriage does to you, I don't want

to get married!" He laughed at his joke, and I forced a smile.

It's really not funny.

Something was very wrong.

෧෧෧෧

Shortly after Denise and I got married, I came down with a bad case of the flu. I could no longer lie down because the sensation of my lungs filling up with phlegm made it impossible to sleep. Months into our marriage, I moved out of our bedroom and into the recliner in the living room, where I could at least drift in and out of sleep in a sitting position.

Denise and I had moved to Carson City, Nevada, where she got a job for a tile company, and I worked in a restaurant and kept unnatural hours. I woke up at 4 a.m. to drive an hour to my 5:30 a.m. shift in the kitchen. I did grab an extra bite of food here and there on the job, but it didn't seem like enough to justify how tight my clothes had become.

Even stranger, the less I ate the more weight I gained. I usually threw together a peanut butter and jelly sandwich for breakfast, but the flu made me throw it up. Eventually the only food I could keep down was a sugar doughnut, and I had one every day. When I couldn't keep the doughnuts down anymore, I went into a forced fast from food altogether.

I could barely function through my shifts at the

restaurant. My group had agreed to combine the three short breaks we were allotted into one hour-long break, during which I propped myself up in the corner of a couch in the employee lounge and slept. If a co-worker hadn't tapped me on the shoulder at the end of the hour to wake me up, I probably would have been out all day.

The guys in the restaurant noticed my rapid weight gain, although some found it as mysterious as I did.

"Are you body building?" one co-worker asked me, looking down at my lower legs that were bulging over the tops of my socks. "Lord! I've never seen calves that size."

I leaned over to check them out myself.

"You're right! I've never seen them that big, either."

But I wasn't working out. I wasn't riding my bicycle several hundred miles a month like I'd done before Denise and I got married.

I wasn't doing anything except dragging myself to work, sleeping in an upright position, throwing up everything I tried to eat or drink and getting fat.

I needed to get this under control.

ॐॐॐ

The Monday morning after my brother's weekend visit, I drove myself to the doctor.

"I'm having this flu thing," I told him, listing off my symptoms. "I can't lay down at night, the weight is piling on and I'm not even eating that much. I think I need to get on some kind of weight loss system."

The doctor nodded his head slightly.

"I don't think it's so much of a nutrition problem or needing a little more exercise."

"But that's got to be part of it. All I was eating for weeks was sugar doughnuts, and now I can't even drink a glass of water without getting sick."

"Look, Dan, I'm going to order some blood work. I need you to stay home from work and rest until the results come back. It will probably take about two days. Call me on Wednesday, and we can talk more about it when I have more information."

I tried not to roll my eyes. Was he kidding? Stay home from work? If I could get up and go, I needed to get up and go.

Missing work meant losing income, so I worked my shifts on Tuesday and Wednesday.

"Dan?"

The doctor hadn't waited for me to call.

"The blood work is back, and this is probably something a little more serious than you thought. I need you to come in to my office."

❧❧❧

The words "end stage renal disease" reverberated through the room like an echo in a canyon.

My face was blank.

"Doctor, I don't even know what that is."

"It's kidney failure, and you're in the last stage of it. There's no fixing what you have."

He'd already reserved a room for me in a hospital in Reno.

"You need to pick up your wife and drive there immediately. Don't go back to work, and don't run any errands that would waste time."

He forced me to look him in the eyes. "Get in your car, and go to the hospital. Now."

"Okay, doc." I numbly took the information he pressed into my hands and headed for the parking lot.

This is crazy. I've got to get a second opinion, see another doctor. I am 20 years old! This doesn't happen to 20 year olds. That doctor is out of his mind.

My body, however, agreed with the doctor. I worked my shifts on Thursday and Friday, but my vomiting became so frequent that I could hardly function. I couldn't keep food or liquid down, and the lack of nourishment was making me pale and sickly.

I never did get a second opinion. I did, however, finally tell my wife.

"Denise, I'm sick."

She looked at me calmly, clearly already knowing this.

"The doctor called it 'end stage renal disease.' He wants me to go to the hospital in Reno."

Denise picked up her purse and keys. "Why aren't we at the hospital already if they can fix this?"

I had no fight left in me. My head lolled against the passenger side window as Denise drove through the barren Nevada landscape to Reno. I stared blankly, sometimes dozing, as my body began to give out.

INSIDE OUT

❧❧❧

"Hi, I'm Dan Loflin. My doctor said something about a room would be waiting for me here?"

The receptionist put down her pen.

"Did you say your name was Dan Loflin?" She bounced out of her seat and around her desk to grab my arm gently. "Where have you been? We've had a room waiting for you for days!"

She passed me to a nurse, who quickly measured my weight, height and blood pressure. The nurse led me to a hospital bed, and I was passed out before my head settled onto the pillow.

❧❧❧

My eyes slowly opened to a new space-age reality. The hospital room pulsed with beeping machines connected to me through a web of tubes and wires. I pushed my chin down to look at my chest, where a large catheter horrifyingly protruded.

I looked up at Denise.

What's going on?

Where am I?

What is this machine?

The questions poured out of me in waves, fueled by the fear growing in my gut. I'd never before been sick, certainly not badly enough to be in the hospital.

How long have I been asleep?!

Have I had surgery?

When do I get out of here?

"It's going to be a while," Denise said, stroking my hand. "It's going to be longer than we expected. You're hooked up to a dialysis machine, which is cleaning the toxins out of your body because your kidneys aren't working."

The nephrologist offered more detail, although not more than he thought I needed. My kidneys had been failing, which had resulted in my body filling with toxins and fluids it could no longer extract from my system. My lungs were so saturated with liquid there was little room for air, and my body-builder calves were all water.

"You'll need to go on dialysis, probably for the rest of your life." If I could have sat up in shock, I would have. "You'll go to the dialysis center every other day, and it will take about three to four hours to clean out your system. You'll get used to it, and soon it will become a regular part of your life."

My brain continued to scream questions. *What about my job? What does this mean for the rest of my life? Is this my only option?*

According to this doctor, it was. Dialysis was a known and reliable procedure that he recommended for people with serious, chronic kidney issues.

❧❧❧

I walked out of the hospital a month later, 60 pounds lighter thanks to dialysis cleaning the extra fluid out of my body. I could breathe and walk easier. Thankfully I still had a job, although I had to alternate working days with dialysis days. I'd been a good employee, and my boss was willing to keep me on the schedule with reduced hours.

Dialysis was a roller coaster of ups and downs, good and bad, sick and well. I'd leave treatments feeling horrible, but within a few hours I'd feel back to normal. Then I had to watch what I ate and drank so that I wouldn't retain too much fluid between dialysis visits. By the time I returned to the clinic, I was full of toxins, tired and sick.

This was not going to work for me. One look around the dialysis clinic was all I needed.

People lay quietly on chairs, hooked up to machines that filtered their blood. The machines might as well have sucked the life out of them, too, as it looked to me like they'd given up. Their faces appeared dull and gray, empty of life and hope. They dragged themselves in and out of the clinic, like longtime factory workers headed in and out of another grueling shift. I was always one of the youngest people in the room, and I didn't like the future that I saw there.

With a little research, I found a transplant clinic in San Francisco.

The doctor gave me the pros and cons of a transplant. My body could reject a new kidney. Or, it could accept the organ, and I could live dialysis-free for 10 to 15 years.

For me, the answer was obvious.

PERFECT MATCH

❧❧❧❧

John and I were rolled into the operating room together, our beds parallel. A nurse stood at our feet, rubbing her temple with the end of her pen.

"Now, you're receiving, and you're giving, right?" She pointed the pen at John.

"No!" My brother laughed, although we knew the cost of such an error could be fatal. "Dan's getting my kidney, not the other way around."

This was the third time a nurse had made this mistake. John was exactly two years younger than me and a little blonder and taller. Lying on hospital beds, however, we looked similar.

"We've got to get this right." The nurse taped a large piece of paper over each of our beds and wrote "GIVING" on John's and "RECEIVING" on mine.

John's kidney was a good match for me, and he had been willing to give it to me when the transplant clinic asked about potential sibling donors. In those days, doctors wouldn't even consider half-siblings or strangers, so John was my only option.

I had spent several months prior to the transplant in an experimental program where doctors used radiation to deaden my lymph nodes, which they said should make my body confused enough about the new kidney that it wouldn't reject it.

The six weeks of radiation paid off. I walked out of the hospital 10 days after the operation feeling like I could run a marathon, and within a week of discharge, I was walking two miles a day. The shortness of breath and rundown feeling disappeared, thanks to my brother's kidney.

❧❧❧

Denise and I carried on with our lives. We moved back to the Portland area to be closer to our families, and I worked hard at another restaurant. But 18 months after the transplant, my body began to wake up from the radiation treatments and realize there was a foreign object inside it.

For months, something hadn't felt right to me, but I didn't really have any specific complaints or symptoms. My doctors assured me my blood work looked fine, but I decided to move to another clinic, and I took my paperwork with me.

Before I gave the records to my new doctor, I took a look. For the prior six months, doctors had made notations that my kidney was failing, but because I wasn't complaining about symptoms, there would be no change in protocol.

"Yes, you're right," my new doctor told me. "That kidney will fail eventually, but we'll treat it as long as we can. Then you'll need another transplant."

My potassium levels finally shot high enough that the doctor sent me to the dialysis clinic. An overload of potassium, which the kidneys typically clean from the system, can make your heart stop.

I've never liked needles, and no matter how many times I visited the dialysis clinic, I always turned my head when the nurse put the needle in my arm. Plus, going to the clinic took up as many hours as a part-time job, so I opted for a more mobile form of dialysis that allowed me to clean out my own system without needles or clinic visits.

Doctors ran a permanent tube into my abdomen that settled between my stomach lining and outside cavity. Every four hours, except when I was asleep at night, I would lean over so that fluid inside my stomach would drain out. Then, I'd use the tube to pour in a new bag of fluid, which would absorb the toxins in my body. The process required enough medical supplies to fill an entire room in our apartment.

Home dialysis allowed me to keep working full time. I needed to exchange fluids twice during a restaurant shift, which I did in the basement employee locker room. To keep my co-workers from thinking I was lazy or taking too many breaks, I'd cut a few corners in the process. I stopped microwaving the fluid bags to bring them to body temperature, which saved me a few minutes.

One night after an on-the-job fluid exchange, my side began to ache like I'd consumed too much water before going for a run. By the time I got home at 11 p.m., I was so buckled over in pain that I shuffled to the front door like the hunchback of Notre Dame. I knocked on the door, and Denise walked me back to the car and drove me to the hospital, where I was treated for an infection of the stomach cavity. My cold-fluid exchanges in the unsanitary locker room had done me in.

I lashed out at God, who I had hardly acknowledged up until then. In fact, I really didn't believe in him.

Why me? I've been a good kid my whole life. I stayed out of trouble and have tried to do the right thing. What have I done to deserve this?

I didn't drink. I didn't smoke. I ate a healthy diet to ease the workload on my kidney. But still I got sick.

I made a decision.

If none of that matters, then nothing matters.

❧❧❧

I took up drinking and smoking and partying. I worked swing shifts and stayed out all night with my co-workers, who became like a big family of unhealthy people. We often sat around for hours, having pseudo-deep conversations fueled by alcohol.

Often, our conversations revolved around our religious beliefs — or lack thereof.

"I don't know what I believe," I boldly proclaimed one night. "But if there is a hell, I'll let you know what it's like when I get there."

My other favorite topics included "God Doesn't Exist" and "Love Isn't Real," my subject matter reflecting my new, dark perspective.

Life, after all, was just for today, and I planned to have as much fun as possible.

Sometimes well-intentioned friends would gently ask if drinking and smoking was good for me, considering I was living with a transplanted, failing kidney. "I don't care," was my standard response.

Denise gave birth to our daughter, but having a new baby didn't curb my partying. I figured if my shift ended at 11 p.m. and it took me an hour to drive home, they'd be asleep. At that point, it didn't matter if I got home at midnight or 5 a.m.

But Denise cared, and even her patience rubbed thin. She moved back in with her parents, telling me that if I was going to choose the party lifestyle, she was going to leave. She and her mom packed up Denise's stuff while I was at work.

A knock came on the door around 4 a.m. a few days later. I heaved myself off the couch and wobbled over to the window, horrified to see my father-in-law standing at the door.

Extremely drunk, I opened the door for him. He strode into the room, a raincoat pulled over the suit he wore for the business meeting he was flying to later that day. His hands were jammed in his pockets, probably to keep from hitting me.

He had a pronouncement.

"You know, when you got married, it was for life. She's not happy, you're not happy and you need to figure out how to get back on track."

He didn't wait for a response. Like a mysterious spirit, he swept out of the door and into the night.

INSIDE OUT

∾∾∾

Denise and I started dating again. I tried to stop drinking. We bought a house, and I made a genuine effort to pull my family back together.

Neither of us wanted to divorce or admit that we couldn't make it. A month after Denise left, she and our daughter moved back in.

I hid the drinking from my doctor, who started to talk about another transplant. Transplant technology had advanced enough by then that my half-sister was an eligible donor, and she was willing and had passed the initial medical and psychological tests.

As I dozed in an anesthesia-induced sleep before the surgery, Denise hovered over me. She knew I was groggy.

"You need to start thinking of something other than yourself," I heard her say through the cloud of fog in my head. "Did you ever think about God?"

I woke up hours later thinking about God, mostly that there wasn't one.

I felt great, and I was discharged within a week.

Again, life quickly settled back into a normal routine. After our son was born, we decided that Denise would stay home with the kids. At the same time, I got a salary increase that covered the loss of her income, so we bought the house in the country we'd always wanted.

Life at home with little kids soon got lonely for Denise, so she joined a group at a church down the road called Tuesday Morning Break. The church offered childcare while the moms got together, and soon Denise was a church regular on Tuesdays and Sundays.

She regularly asked me to go to church with her, but I always said no. Sometimes I'd schedule myself for Sunday shifts so I'd have a ready excuse.

Denise finally brought the church to me. Her pastor came to our house for a visit, and we met regularly for six weeks. He talked to me about God and Jesus, and he explained that if I believed in God and asked him to forgive me for all of the things I had done wrong, I could be "saved." According to him, that meant I could have a relationship with God forever.

I could see that this relationship with God was something that I needed — and wanted. But why would Jesus want to be friends with someone who had once loudly proclaimed that he didn't exist? Could God accept a guy who endangered his life and lied to his wife just to have a drink?

ॐॐॐ

The pastor's words echoed in my head that Sunday morning.

You don't have to be perfect. You don't have to clean your life up to have a relationship with God. He will help you get your life in order if you let him.

My insides burned with the desire to answer a call to go to the front of the church at the end of the service. All I had to do was step into the aisle and walk to the front, where a church leader would help me talk to God and ask him to start a relationship.

I felt like everyone in church knew that the pastor and I had talked about me "getting saved," and this was the Sunday I was supposed to make it official. As the music played at the end of the service and the pastor invited people to come to the front, I only gripped the chair in front of me harder.

Denise tapped me with her elbow and swiveled her chin toward the front.

I know I'm supposed to go up there today. I just can't.

Then it seemed like every face in the church was staring at me, waiting.

How can I be part of this church full of perfect people? If they knew where I've been and what I've done, they wouldn't want me around here.

It took me another week to let go of the seat and walk forward. I believed that God loved me like I was. I just had to accept it.

Later that morning, I was baptized in a pool of water. The pastor lowered me under the water and then out of it, symbolizing that I was a new person because I was in a relationship with God.

I didn't feel that new, however. I was slowly changing, but I had a long way to go. I joined a men's group, which met weekly to talk about the Bible and about our own lives. The men in my group were brutally honest, and they opened up about issues that ranged from infidelity to alcoholism. We talked weekly about how we could be better husbands to our wives. For the first time, I saw that I wasn't the only one who'd messed up. God loved all of us, including me.

❧❧❧

When I opened my eyes, the black world outside my truck's windshield was upside down.

What has happened to me? Where am I?

The night outside was still, the quiet broken only by the sound of an insect or frog. The last I remembered, I'd stayed a little late after work with my friends and drunk a little more than I should have before I got in the truck for the hour-long drive home.

I tested my limbs, moving around the best I could while hanging upside down in a seatbelt. Nothing hurt, and nothing seemed to be bleeding. I'd somehow flipped my truck into a ditch without inflicting a scratch upon myself.

Before I got down, God had something to say. I *heard* his voice cut through the cold night air.

This is the day you are going to make a choice and get off the fence. You can't say you are choosing me but continue to choose your old life.

My mind flashed back to a night in the bar with a guy from work. "Do you really believe in this church stuff?" he asked, eyeing my beer. From his viewpoint, my getting involved in "church stuff" hadn't changed a thing about the way I behaved after work.

INSIDE OUT

I wriggled out of the seatbelt and lowered myself onto the ceiling of my truck's cab, which was now the floor. The gifts I'd bought Denise for Valentine's Day lay scattered. I gathered them up and began the 15-mile trek home along the shoulder of the dark road while I continued the conversation God had started.

Could I really stop drinking? Was it possible for me to change? I'd been arrested twice for drunk driving and gone through rehab only to quickly fall back into drinking.

I took a deep breath, shivering in the cold as I walked.

Okay, God. That's it. Tonight is the end of my old life.

A car pulled up beside me, scattering gravel on the shoulder of the road. The passenger side window was down.

"Hey, can I give you a ride?" the driver called to me.

I nodded and slipped into the seat. We sat in silence as we drove the 15 miles to my house, and I quietly let myself in.

My life changed that night. Old patterns were broken instantly. I could say no to a night out after work. Beer and liquor had no appeal. I came home on time, sobered up and became an involved husband and father.

తతతత

Deciding to follow God affected my home life and my business choices. After my night in the truck, I no longer felt like I was on the same page as the others at the restaurant. I eventually took a job at a food service company.

While sitting in a company meeting with 300 people one day, a guy got up on stage and announced that the company was opening an office in Central Oregon. Denise and I had always wanted to move there, where the climate was dry and there were plenty of lakes for water skiing.

"Hey, I'm interested in that position in Central Oregon," I told the guy after the meeting.

"What are you talking about?"

"You have a position open in Central Oregon. You just announced it from the stage."

"But I haven't said anything about it yet."

"I was sitting right there in the meeting, and you said it in front of everyone."

I got a blank stare in return. *Am I the only one who heard him say that?*

With that inside information, I quickly interviewed for the job and was offered the position. Our kids, then in seventh and ninth grade, were surprisingly in favor of the move. Denise and I downsized into a small house on 5 acres out in the country, and the smaller mortgage freed me up to work less and spend more time traveling and volunteering at our new church, Eastside.

Then, my 15 years on my half-sister's kidney were up.

It started with leg cramps at night, caused by dehydration as salts built up in my body. When I played with a men's softball league, I could barely make it to first base. The doctor gave me as much medication as he could, but it wasn't enough to allow me to function normally on a failing kidney.

INSIDE OUT

I called John.

"What do you think about giving me that other kidney?"

My brother was always good for a joke when life got serious. "Yeah, I think I'll have to say no this time."

The symptoms of kidney failure were familiar. The lack of anxiety in the face of it, however, was not.

Death was no longer scary, because I trusted that I'd be with God whether I was alive or dead. If it was time for me to go home to heaven, I was ready. Whatever the future held, I could take a deep breath, let it out and let God take over.

When the time came for me to get back on dialysis, doctors reinserted a tube in my arm and a catheter in my upper chest. My doctor in Portland, who I'd continued to see for years, kept my blood work on file to compare with potential donor kidneys. He wasn't optimistic about a match, though, because my body had built up so many antibodies that it likely would reject most kidneys. He advised me that my wait would probably be at least three years.

❧❧❧

For some reason, I carried my transplant pager with me even though the signal from Portland couldn't really reach Central Oregon. The doctor had told me to keep it on me at all times, so I did out of habit. Plus, there was always that unlikely *just in case* scenario.

36

One morning as I was finishing paperwork at my desk at home, I remembered I'd left the pager in the car.

I should go out and get it.

Why? I asked myself. *That's silly. It's never going to go off.*

I made the quick trip to the car and got it, anyway, then set it in front of me on the desk.

Beep-beep! Beep-beep!

I looked up. *Was that the pager? I wonder if they are testing it.*

I called the transplant clinic, anyway. The nurse answered.

"Hi, this is Dan Loflin. My pager just went off, and I'm just calling to find out if everything's okay with it."

"I didn't call you," the nurse said, sounding confused.

"You're right," I said, releasing my sliver of hope for an available kidney like a helium balloon. "This must be a fluke."

"Hold on a minute," she said as I was about to hang up. "Don't go anywhere. I'll call you back in a minute."

The next five minutes felt like five years. Finally, the phone rang. It was the surgeon.

"There's been a death in Florida that's opened up a kidney that's a good match for you."

The chances of this happening had been miniscule. My heart leapt.

"Denise!" I screamed, running through the house trying to find her. "We've got to go to Portland! They have a kidney for me!"

I had been prepped for dialysis, but the call came before the first needle was stuck into my arm. I believed it was a sign that everything was going to be fine. God, I felt, was showing me his love through this amazingly quick match.

❧❧❧

I went into surgery on a Friday and walked out of the hospital three days later with my new kidney. I went right back to work, and my boss never had to find anyone to work my job during my anticipated three years on dialysis.

My children were teenagers, with one close to high school graduation, but Denise and I felt far from ready to be empty nesters.

We weren't finished with family life yet, so we started thinking about adoption. Our kids encouraged us — my daughter said she thought we'd be good adoptive parents. We had extra bedrooms and extra love.

The process took two and a half years, starting with us sifting through hundreds of pictures of available kids. We wanted a school-age brother and sister and expressed interest in several sibling pairs.

In our county, three sets of potential parents were pitched to a committee for each child. We were told several times that we were finalists, only to learn that another set of parents had been chosen. Each time, the sadness felt as weighty as that of a miscarriage as we mourned the children we'd lost.

Anya and Jack were our last hope. When we were told we were the second choice, we booked two tickets for a much-needed vacation to Mexico.

Then the phone rang.

"We want to talk to you about Anya and Jack," the social worker began. We had desperately wanted these children, and it hurt to hear their names again. "You really were the second choice. We weren't just saying that. Their first placement didn't work out, and we are wondering if you are still interested in them."

"Well, my wife and I are about to leave for Cabo for a vacation. I'm not sure if we could go through the process right away."

"That's not a problem. You take your vacation, and you can meet Anya and Jack when you get back."

We went to Cabo and vacationed on the beach, but all we talked about was Anya and Jack. Every day we were away, our excitement grew at the possibility of two children waiting for us when we got home.

Within a month, they were our son and daughter. We may have been the adoption agency's second choice parents for these beautiful children, but in our hearts we knew that God had perfectly matched us. We were God's *first choice* parents.

৵৵৵

In 2009, my annual blood work showed that my third transplanted kidney was failing quickly, and in June, I was put on dialysis three times a week for three hours a session.

This time there were no physical symptoms. I had been feeling fine, and I was shocked at the blood work.

Even worse, by then my antibodies were sensitized to 98 percent of the population. My doctor said I should prepare for a lifetime of dialysis, as there likely would never be another transplant match.

In the past, Denise and I had always had a plan when my kidneys failed. I'd do a few months of dialysis, quickly get a transplant and life would resume as normal. This time, that plan was not in play. The doctor was hesitant to even put me on the transplant list.

As I stood in church one morning, my anxiety level got so high that it felt like it was spilling over. I felt like God spoke to me again.

I will take care of you. Open your hands.

I slowly uncurled my fingers and felt the cool air on my palms.

Relax. Let this go. I don't want you to think about this anymore. I don't want you to pray for healing anymore, because I am giving you the answer. I am going to heal you.

God, what do I do?

Go about your life. Stop being anxious. Keep getting treatment, but know that your healing will be taken care of.

I sat down on the chair as a warm peace flowed through my body. I didn't know how this healing would happen, but I was sure that God had it under control. For so long, I had been so concerned about my health that I hadn't cared about other people the way I should have. It was time to change.

❦❦❦

I embraced what once scared me. In particular, Disneyland.

Anya and Jack's first set of adoptive parents had promised them a trip there, and Denise and I wanted to honor that promise even though neither of us liked the place. For me, the trip meant added anxiety of having to dialyze in a strange place. I preferred the familiarity of the clinic at home, where I knew the routine and the nurses.

But I wanted to show the kids that life went on. I was sick, but I wasn't going to let that stop me. When this family faced illness, or any crisis for that matter, we stuck together.

That trip led to more trips, and I visited dialysis clinics all over the country. I knew that God had a plan for me and had promised to take care of me, so it was easier to let go of anxiety and enjoy life despite my alarming health issues.

Some research uncovered a medical trial at Stanford University where doctors were administering a treatment for people with antibody buildup. The doctors added me to the list and gave me infusions to lower my antibodies. I marveled that a match could even be possible. In my decades with kidney disease, they had progressed from only transplanting kidneys from full siblings to having the ability to transplant kidneys from stranger to stranger.

I tried the treatment for several months, but blood work indicated that I was still 98 percent sensitized to antibodies. The doctor wanted to try a more aggressive approach, and if it failed, I'd no longer be eligible for the treatment.

After my first treatment, I went in for my regular dialysis appointment. Needles still bothered me, so I had taught myself to sleep for the three-hour treatment.

The phone rang half an hour before my session ended, jarring me awake. It was a Stanford phone number.

Probably another doctor calling with bad news. I just talked to them a few days ago. How much do they expect one patient to take?

I glumly answered the call.

"Hey!" It was a cheerful nurse. "I think we have a match for you, but we need to know if you are willing to drive down here. Are you available for a possible transplant?"

Are you kidding me? Of course I'm available!

"I can be there in three hours."

"Don't do anything. I'll call you right back."

That meant I had one minute to get myself unhooked from the machine and get dressed.

"Nurse! I've got to get off dialysis now! Right now!"

"What do you mean? You're almost finished."

This could be my last time on dialysis ever, and I couldn't get that needle out of my arm fast enough.

"They might have a kidney for me at Stanford. I have to go now!"

The phone rang again as the nurse disentangled me from the machine that had become my regular companion for three years. In my mind, the machine and I had already broken up.

"Yes, we'll have the kidney here," the nurse on the phone said. "Come down as quickly as you can."

For the first time in my life, my blood didn't clot well when the nurse removed the dialysis needles, and as I flailed around trying to get myself out the door, blood squirted all over me like an off-screen murder in a horror movie. The nurse rushed over and tried to re-bandage my arm while I dialed my wife's number.

"I've got to get out of here!"

The nurse was thinking a little more rationally.

"Dan, you cannot get on a plane covered in bodily fluids." I looked down at my shirt that by then resembled a red Jackson Pollack painting. "Here, wear these."

I threw on the extra set of scrubs from the nurse and headed to the airport, which was half a mile away. The quickest way the airline could get me to San Francisco was almost seven hours at a cost of $1,200.

"Don't you have a bereavement fare?" I was beyond desperate.

"That fare is only available if someone has died," the airline desk attendant calmly replied.

"Really? No one's going to die, but I need to get to San Francisco now!"

Pending transplant patients apparently were not eligible for reduced fares, so I headed back to the car. I could drive to Stanford in seven hours. Denise met me on the way out of town, and we rode together toward what was looking like a miracle.

૨૦૨૦૨૦

The kidney took its time getting from Boston to San Francisco. It missed its first flight when someone forgot to put the cooler on the plane, and then it enjoyed a layover in Las Vegas before finally making its way to California.

As the kidney traveled across the country, I fasted from food in case I was called into surgery and checked in and out of the hospital as its arrival was repeatedly delayed.

"Hey, are you the guy getting the Las Vegas kidney?" one ultrasound technician asked. "I hear it stopped over for one last fling before the transplant."

I could hardly laugh, as any humor was shrouded with worry that the kidney wouldn't be viable for transplant when it finally arrived. The doctor had said the kidney was from an older person, and at age 48, I was wondering, *How much older?*

Any chance, though, was better than nothing.

The blood work between me and the kidney aligned, and doctors inserted the Las Vegas kidney just below my stomach. The surgery took an extra two hours because doctors had to find room for it among all of the other kidneys that were still in my body. Doctors usually don't remove failing kidneys — they stack the new one on top.

The kidney was functioning the day of the surgery, and within hours, I was using the bathroom.

God did as I believe he promised. He took care of me.

৵৵৵

During my three years of dialysis, the people at Eastside Church often asked how they could pray for me.

I would say, "You don't need to. How can I pray for you?" I believed God told me not to dwell on my own problems because he would heal me, and I embraced my freedom to focus on other people.

I remained so thankful for the friends we made at Eastside and the support we got through Bible studies and small groups of foster and adoptive parents.

When I was wracked with anxiety, Eastside Church gave me somewhere else to focus.

At age 50, I felt better than I did at 24. I worked full time. Denise and I were parenting two young kids. I liked to water ski. I could walk 18 holes of golf. I hiked.

God replaced my anger and depression and tendency to ask "why me?" with a miraculous peace and trust.

And a perfect-match kidney.

WHOLLY BROKEN
The Story of Thomas
Written by Sharon Kirk Clifton

My eyelids flew open. I lay motionless on my bed, daring not even to breathe as I listened in the night. What had jerked me out of a sound sleep? I heard nothing but normal neighborhood noises — a dog barking in the distance, crickets chirping in the sultry night. Neither of which would have disturbed my sleep. Had I locked the doors? Of course. That was routine. I was alone.

No, I wasn't. I could sense another presence. The room held very little ambient light, but I felt an inky darkness hover over me, darker than the rest of the room. It began to take shape. I recognized the face, though it had twisted from the happy little visage I knew so well into something grotesque and malevolent.

My heart pounded against the walls of my chest, and a deep aching dread snaked its way through my gut. A fear such as I'd never before known gripped me.

I needed help, but who could help me?

"No," I heard myself whimper. "Leave me. I do not belong to you anymore."

It had been a week since I'd mailed the letter. They must have received it.

એએએ

INSIDE OUT

"Have a seat wherever you want, boys." Midge, the 50-something owner of The Cookie Cutter, gave a sweeping gesture around the little eatery. "I gotta get these cookies out of the oven before they become burnt offerings."

Bill led the way to the little, round glass-topped table back in one corner. "Smells like chocolate chip, Midge."

"Yep. You know your cookies." She pulled the huge cookie sheet from the oven and set it down on the back counter before turning to take our order. "So what can I get for you, gents? Soups today are broccoli cheese, black bean and French onion."

"Good as those sound, Midge," Bill said, "think I'll go with the usual, garlic-cheese bread and black coffee."

Midge put her hands on her hips and shook her head. "I declare, Bill. You're in a deep rut." Then she looked my way and smiled. "And how about you?"

"I'm in the rut with Bill, but make it a Coke, instead of coffee."

Bill was quiet for a moment, absentmindedly scratching at his beard and tugging at his bushy mustache. Finally, he looked up at me with his clear blue eyes. "You given any thought to what we talked about the last time we met?"

I rested my arms on the table. "We talked about a lot of things. Like always. What specifically?" Even as I asked the question, I knew exactly what he meant.

"About your dad."

"You're my dad."

"You know what I mean. Your birth father. About

48

reconnecting with him. Reconciling your differences."

"Yeah, I've thought some about it."

"Good. And?"

"And … I don't see it happening. He threatened to kill me, Bill! What man threatens to kill his own son?"

"He wasn't in his right mind."

"And he is now? Bill, he never was in his right mind. The booze, the drugs, the women — they control him. He never cared one bit about his family."

Bill leaned in, resting on his forearms. "I understand that. Believe me, I *do* understand. Remember, I lived with an abusive, alcoholic father, too. Which is exactly why I'm telling you to consider at least making an effort at reconciliation. I never did, and I regret that. Now, he's gone."

"Here ya go, gentlemen." Midge set our drinks in front of us, sloshing a bit of the steaming hot coffee from Bill's cup. She quickly grabbed a napkin from the pocket of her apron and wiped it up. "Be right back with the rest."

"The smell of those cookies is killing me," I said. "Why don't you bring us a couple of them, too? Put 'em on my ticket."

"No problem." She grinned and winked. "Gotcha, didn't I?" She soon returned with our food.

As soon as she was out of earshot, Bill leaned in again. "I'm not going to push you, son. It's a decision you have to make. You've gone through some major changes in your life, too, some things you might want to share with him."

"I need to think about it some more."

He broke off a piece of cookie. "I hope you'll do more than just think about it." He smiled and stuffed the cookie chunk in his mouth.

❧❧❧

The thought of talking to my real dad, let alone actually meeting with him, sickened me. When I turned my back on him and fled from that hospital room back in 1991, I determined never to have anything to do with him again, though in my darkest moments, my mind still replayed the stream of curse words he spewed in my wake.

Including his threats to kill me.

Why would I want to reconcile with a man who had poisoned the lives of everyone around him? Someone, some sympathetic sap, might say he was a victim of a familial propensity toward alcoholism. After all, as I was being born on the OB floor of a hospital in Berkeley, California, Dad's mother lay dying of cirrhosis of the liver, the result of her own lifelong addiction to booze.

In 1970, when I was 1 year old, my brother was born. Two years later, Mom divorced my father. She later told us boys it was because of his drinking, as well as his being a husband and father *in absentia.* It would be a while before we learned why he spent so much time away from home.

Mom remarried in 1973. Our stepfather, Greg, kept a tight rein on my brother and me, which was a good thing, though we didn't see it that way growing up. Our half-brother Jeff was born in 1974.

Greg, my stepfather, considered family very

important. I admired that about him. He treated my brother and me decent, though as kids, we thought he was pretty tough on us. He demanded respect and expected us to obey.

Money was always a problem, though. There wasn't much of it, and Greg often wasted what little we had on drink. He, too, was an alcoholic. My brothers and I spent many nights in his truck waiting for him to get done drinking inside some bar.

One night, he was so bombed that he could barely keep the truck on the road going home. After he crashed into a friend's mailbox, demolishing it, he made us get out and walk up two miles of mountain road to where we were living at the time. No one said a word on that trek. Greg was doing well to put one foot in front of the other and keep going in the general direction of forward. Patrick, Jeff and I were too tired. The full moon lit our way, and the crickets sang us home.

The next morning, Greg woke up wondering where his truck was. We told him it was down the mountain in the road.

During our growing-up years, Patrick and I spent summers with Dad — well, really, with his Aunt Millie. He lived with her, too, off and on, when he wasn't cohabiting with one of his string of girlfriends or off on a drunken binge. His aunt had basically raised him, since his alcoholic mother was hardly able to take care of herself, let alone her son.

Throughout her life, Aunt Millie had invested much in

real estate. She owned several rental properties, including the apartment complex where she lived, which had a swimming pool. She wasn't exactly wealthy, but she was well-off.

We loved it at Aunt Millie's. She spoiled us rotten. She was widowed with no children, so she lavished us with gifts and privileges as if we were her grandchildren. Summers were a flurry of camping trips in her Winnebago to visit ghost towns, monuments, museums and other sites, long days of our playing in the pool while she sat on the side doing her accounting for her rental business, and going to movies and getting ice cream whenever Dad was sober enough to take us. We had more toys than we ever needed, including a mountain of Legos. Every couple of years we went to Disneyland. Oh, yeah, life was good with Aunt Millie!

When I told Mom that Patrick and I wanted to live with Dad and Aunt Millie all year, not just summers, she didn't seem surprised, nor did she try to dissuade us. Instead, she threw up reasons why that was a good idea.

"You're entering your teen years, a time when boys need to be with their father. Your great-aunt loves you very much, and she can do much more for you than Greg and I can. And I know she can feed you growing boys better than we can."

Another reason went unspoken. She and Greg were not getting along well. I had heard their voices raised in anger.

Aunt Millie was thrilled to have us with her full time,

and she had plenty of room in her large apartment. The only problem was she had three bedrooms, not the four she needed for us to each have our own space.

"Aha!" she said. "I'll just confiscate a bedroom from the neighboring apartment before a new tenant moves in." And she did. Dad's bedroom was then the newly added one. The way it had to be configured, though, meant that to get to his room he had to go through mine. Most of the time that was okay, since he spent so much time elsewhere. But when the latest love of his life kicked his rear to the street and he stumbled home drunk or strung out on cocaine, it was not pleasant. I was the one he saw first, so I was the one he yelled and cursed at.

Living with Aunt Millie, I learned more about my father than I ever wanted to know. I heard the arguments they had, usually over money. Hers. She loved him unconditionally. He was a son to her. He took advantage of that. She had no concept of tough love. He was a manipulator. He knew what strings to pull to get her to support his addictions, and he often used Patrick and me, threatening to yank us out of her care and take us to live with him and his latest bimbo. Patrick and I would naturally put up a fuss, since we wanted no part of Dad's nonsense, and Aunt Millie would cave in to his demands for money.

Many times she bore bruises that testified of his physical abuse. He was always able to get what he wanted from her, one way or another. If she didn't give money to him willingly, he stole it.

INSIDE OUT

When I hit 16, I went looking for work. My starter job was with a small bakery, but within a year, I was working at a local drugstore. I had a great boss, Ezra, a Jewish man whose round, rosy cheeks made him look like a young Santa Claus. He soon figured out my home life sucked, and he began mentoring me. It wasn't long before he promoted me to supervisor. For a while, I tried juggling high school with working 40 hours a week. That didn't go well. I started oversleeping mornings. My studies suffered. By my senior year, I was earning double minimum wage, so I dropped out of school.

Life at home was getting worse. Dad had split with the latest girlfriend, so he spent a lot of time at home. The drinking and drug use intensified, and as they did, his anger and abusiveness got worse.

Furthermore, Aunt Millie began showing signs of Alzheimer's. The more independent I became, earning my own money to take care of my needs, the more I resented him for leeching off of her.

A year after leaving high school, I realized I needed to do something more with my life, so I signed up to take the California High School Proficiency Exam and passed it. I was thrilled. At home, the news was met with total indifference. Neither my dad nor my great-aunt offered a "congratulations" or "good job."

Undeterred, I signed up for classes at Diablo Valley Community College, paying for it all myself. The first semester went well. My grades were good, and I was still working full time. As life at home got crazier still, my second semester's grades plummeted. My dad's affinity for alcohol, cocaine and prostitutes grew out of control, Aunt Millie sank deeper into the abyss of her disease and I felt my life go into a tailspin. I needed help, but I didn't know where to find it.

છે છે છે

Deepak Sandifar, a regular customer at the pharmacy, was a tall man whose easy smile reached his eyes. There was a certain gentleness about him, and he was intentional with his words.

One day he came in, took one look at me and asked if everything was okay. I must have looked worried or stressed.

I started to say everything was fine, but the man seemed to really care, so I admitted that my life was in a downward spiral, and I felt totally out of control.

"Can you break away from here for a little bit? Go for some pizza?"

"I shouldn't ... Sure, why not?"

We went to a little neighborhood pizzeria. The server brought us our Cokes, and we put in our order.

Deepak took a long draw on his straw before saying anything. "Thomas, I haven't lived out here long. Back East, I was a licensed counselor, but I haven't gone through the application process here, yet. However, I'd be happy to help in any way I can, if you want to talk."

His invitation started an avalanche of words and pain.

When had I ever had anyone care to hear anything I had to say, aside from at work and school? I felt validated in those places but certainly not at home. Yet here was a relative stranger who listened with his whole being. When I had talked it all out, Deepak offered another invitation.

"I am Hindu, Thomas. And I would like for you to come with me to the temple."

In early summer of 1990, I went with Deepak to the Hindu temple in Concord, California. It was in a converted Lutheran church. Shrines to various deities were set up across the front of the church. The scent of sandalwood incense hung in the air.

At first, I felt uncomfortable, but the more I thought about it, the better I liked the idea of the monastic life, of breaking away from all the problems at home, of having time to meditate in serene surroundings. It was enticing.

Shortly following that initial introduction, I got a call from one of the monks asking me to come and partake of the monastic life for six months, a sort of trial period. I put in my notice at work and told my family goodbye.

At the temple, I studied Hinduism and took some basic six-month vows for chastity and obedience. I hadn't been there long before I was invited to go to the main temple and monastery on the island of Kauai, Hawaii. By that time, I felt comfortable with my life as a Hindu monk. The grounds and architectural elements of the Kauai temple were beautiful. I enjoyed my work there as an accountant, and I liked the worship. I felt especially drawn to Muruga, god of warriors and monks.

In December 1990, a group of us prepared for a trip to India. Having completed my basic Hinduism studies, I participated in the Namakarana (naming) ceremony, receiving my Hindu name of Chinmoy Devananda. I legally changed my name. Then we departed for India, where we stayed for four weeks.

That summer, I went home to see my dad. Aunt Millie's health had dramatically worsened so that she was in an assisted living facility. Dad had power of attorney, giving him free access to her assets. At his hand, her money flowed like water through a sieve.

Of course, his many years of hard living were wreaking serious effects on his health. In a few short months, his appearance aged by years. His skin turned sallow and dry, his eyes, glassy.

One night, he was in extremely bad shape. He wasn't eating or drinking anything except whiskey. I think he was trying to drink himself to death. He was dehydrated because of the booze, and he had a fever.

I had to get him to the hospital. Before we went in, he handed me a bag he'd been clutching. "Carry this for me. The hospital told me to bring it." I wasn't sure how that could be, but there wasn't time to discuss it. I had to get him inside.

When the nurse came in to take his vitals, I quietly handed the bag to her.

"What's this?" she said.

"I don't know. Dad insisted that I bring it to the hospital."

She took one look inside and immediately called for help. The bag held a gun. I had never seen my dad with a gun. I didn't know he owned one.

The ER doctor determined he needed to be admitted. That set him off. He freaked out. His imagination ran wild.

"Gimme my bag!" he yelled. There was a scuffle. My father struggled to get free. The hospital staff grabbed him and restrained him. His face was blood red with anger.

He glared at me. "You son of a b****! I'll kill you for this! You hear me? This is all your doing. I'll kill you!"

"He's not well mentally," one of the doctors said. "Needs a psych exam."

I was shaking as I fled the room. I wanted to get out of there, away from the hospital, away from *him,* as quickly as possible. I couldn't even bring myself to think of him as my father. I vowed never to set eyes on him again.

I turned to the only place I could think of. The monastery. I knew the monk who answered the phone, so I told him what had happened. He sent some monks to pick me up. The next day I was on a plane to Kauai for my safety.

సౌసౌసౌ

Spring at the Kauai temple and monastery was glorious. The monks worked long and hard to keep the gardens up to exacting standards. I don't recall ever seeing a weed among the flowers. Golden domes and architectural elements shone in the sunshine. Strategically planted palms provided welcome shade on hot afternoons. The reflection ponds and fountains added to the serenity of the setting. I thought I could stay there forever.

Then one night I had a dream. In it, I was married and had children. I also was a Christian. I couldn't have explained what a Christian was. I just knew that in the dream I was one. The next day, as a fellow monk and I were walking on the grounds, I shared my dream with him. He chuckled. "It was just a dream," he said.

Yes, it was just a dream.

But something changed after that. I became restless at the monastery. *Was this really where I should be? I had come to Hinduism looking for a way to connect with — what? God, whoever he was? Spirituality?*

Yet, no matter how hard I tried — and I did try — I could not learn to meditate as the other monks did. Something got in the way.

Questions flooded my mind. *Did I really want to separate from my blood family? Why couldn't I shake the dream? What would it be like to marry, father children, be a Christian?*

I wanted to see my mom, to talk things over with her. The monks honored my request to leave the monastery and go visit her in Oregon, where she was living by that time. I needed to sort things out.

Mom encouraged me to move to La Grande, Oregon, a scenic valley town of about 13,000 people in the northeast corner of the state. The next day, we headed for La

Grande. I landed a job at JCPenney as a salesclerk. The next day, I found an apartment.

The first day on the job, I met Derek, a young Christian college student from Mississippi.

"Hey, welcome aboard." He told me his name as we shook hands. "And you're?"

"Chinmoy Devananda."

"Say again."

"Chinmoy Devananda. It's my Hindu name."

"You're Hindu?"

"Yep."

"Where you living, man?"

I told him.

"No way! That's where I live. How crazy is that?"

After work, I was tired and just wanted to go home to my little apartment and vegetate. I hadn't put in a full day's work like that in a while. Having lived the monastic life for two years, I was in culture shock, too. I didn't feel like socializing.

Someone knocked on the door. *Probably some kid selling cheese to raise money for new band uniforms. Maybe if I ignore him, he'll go away.* Another knock. I groaned and went to answer it. There stood Derek, wearing a goofy grin and holding out a bag of sweet corn and lugging a watermelon.

"Since you're new in town, I thought y'all might need some fresh produce. How about I show you around the thrivin' metropolis of La Grande?"

"Aw, Derek, man, I'd really like to, but can we make it

another time? I'm wiped out tonight. First day on the new job and all."

"No problem. Hey, me and some of my friends are getting together this weekend to hang out. Don't know what all we'll do. Maybe a movie. I for sure know food'll be involved. Can you join us?"

"That sounds great. Yeah, I'll go with you."

"Cool. Get some rest. Reckon I'll see you at work tomorrow. G'night."

I liked Derek's friends, most of whom were Christians. Of course, I was the only Hindu in the bunch. I started hanging out with them whenever they got together. A young woman named Robin was a part of the group. She was unmarried and expecting a child. We soon started seeing each other apart from the others.

In late summer of 1992, she invited me to meet her family and go to church with them.

That's how I met Bill, Robin's father. He gave me a firm handshake and pulled me in for a hug. I soon learned that was the way he greeted everyone.

"Great to meet you, son. Robin's told us a lot about you."

I went to church with Robin's family regularly after that. The spirituality drew me. Though I had no intention of becoming a Christian, whatever that meant, the relationship Robin's family had with their God piqued my interest.

The church's college group, which was taught by college students, readily accepted me, though I still called myself a Hindu. Many of them, like Robin's family, spoke of Jesus Christ like they knew him personally, as though he was their next-door neighbor or closer — like a brother. He came up in conversation often and easily. That was the kind of relationship I'd hoped for but hadn't found at the monastery. Authentic spirituality.

It didn't take long for Bill and me to become good friends. I had never been treated as well by anyone as Bill treated me. He accepted me, though he didn't accept everything I did, and he made that clear. I thought of him as my dad.

Robin's and my relationship progressed quickly. When I asked Bill for her hand in marriage and said that we wanted to have the wedding in December, he asked that he and I meet and talk at length. We did.

That was when I became acquainted with The Cookie Cutter.

"Chinmoy, I think you know I like you as a person."

"Yes, sir. Thank you."

He nodded, looking me in the eye. "I have to be up front with you."

"Of course. I wouldn't want it any other way."

"As Robin's father, I have to lay down some ground rules before I can give permission for her hand."

I nodded and wondered what was coming.

"First of all, I know you're cohabiting." I felt my face heat up, and I'm pretty sure my heart stopped. "That must cease as of today."

I gave one tentative nod.

"Agreed, son?"

"Yes, sir."

"I must tell you that you will not be permitted to marry in the church, and I think you know why."

"Because I'm Hindu."

"Exactly. While I think very highly of you, I am not thrilled that my little girl is about to be married to someone who does not follow Jesus Christ. That can cause some serious problems in a marriage. But she's of age, so I'm powerless to tell her who she can or cannot wed."

I respected his honesty.

ళళళ

The leaves were turning to shades of autumn and the days were growing short when I had another dream. In it I saw a figure standing with his arms outstretched. He was surrounded by a brilliant light. His eyes seemed to pierce into my spirit. After talking with Bill, I had begun listening closely to the pastor's sermons, so I recognized the figure even before he spoke. He was Jesus Christ. With a voice of authority mingled with great love, he said, "I am Lord."

When I awoke in the morning, the dream remained emblazoned on my mind. One question demanded an answer: *If he is Lord, then what I know is wrong. Doesn't that mean Hinduism is a lie?*

Robin and I married in December, as planned. It was a civil ceremony. We continued to meet with the college group. As the time grew near for the birth of her baby — our baby — a good friend of mine from the group, a guy I called Cowboy, asked me to pray for the coming birth and for the little one. As I began to talk with God, I felt power coursing through me. When I was done, I looked over at Cowboy, who was grinning from ear to ear.

"You ever felt anything like that before?" he said.

I shook my head. How could he possibly know what I had felt? I was afraid to ask.

After the pastor finished preaching on Sunday mornings, he offered an altar call. That was a time when he would ask if anyone in the audience wanted to come to the front of the church for prayer. Most of the people who went up wanted to become followers of Christ.

I had become proficient at distracting myself so that I didn't have to think about what the preacher was saying, but after many slices of garlic-cheese bread and soul-searching conversations with Bill, after long talks with Cowboy and after hearing Jesus himself in my dream proclaim his lordship, I found myself squirming during altar calls.

If he is Lord, then what I know is wrong. Doesn't that mean Hinduism is a lie?

Little Emily was born on February 3, 1993. Robin wanted to have her dedicated on Valentine's Day. The church called it a baby dedication, but it was actually a ceremony committing the parents to raise the child in a Christ-honoring home according to Biblical precepts and committing the church family to support the parents in that effort. I agreed, though I still was officially Hindu. Hindus like ceremonies.

The dedication took place at the beginning of the church service. I stood there as the proud papa, gazing down at our beautiful daughter. Even after we took our seats, I couldn't stop looking at Emily. I couldn't have told anyone the subject of the message.

Then came the altar call. Whatever the pastor had preached on, it must have been impassioned, because tears streamed down his face as he called people to come forward.

All of a sudden, on the other side of the auditorium, a woman stood. The pastor's head jerked in her direction.

"Pastor." Her voice projected to the farthest corner of the auditorium. "There is a young father who needs to come down *here* this morning." She gestured toward the altar where people knelt to pray. Then she sat down.

I knew exactly who she meant. So did many of the people, because they turned to look at me. And she was right. As if someone clicked the "on" switch to a sound recording in my brain, I heard again my long conversations with Bill, chats with Derek and Cowboy and talks with the pastor. I felt God's thumb between my shoulders urging me out of the row and down the aisle.

As I made my way toward the pastor, I spoke to Christ.

"This is it. Here's your chance, Jesus. I know I've broken your law, and I'm so sorry. I want to follow you, Lord. I'm yours." That was my confession of faith.

It was like a whirlwind after church. I had never felt such completeness before.

Of course, everyone was passing Emily around, cooing over her. The congregation celebrated the two births — Emily's first, into our family, and my second, into God's family (John 3:7).

Robin's grandparents, Grandpa and Grandma Morse, gave me a Bible. I began reading it voraciously. Whenever I could find a spare minute, I had my nose in those pages. By late spring, I was in Kings and Chronicles, books that tell about the reigns of the kings of Israel and Judah. I read about how the bad kings made idols and led the people to do the same, but good kings would come to power and tear down the idols. That happened over and over.

Finally, I had an "aha" moment. My Hindu idols were packed away in a box and stashed back in my closet. I needed to destroy them!

I went next door to Derek's apartment.

I flashed him a big grin. "Hey, man, wanna have some fun?"

"What you got in mind?" He gave me a look that said he wouldn't agree to anything until he knew what I was talking about.

"Got any tools? Hammers, mallets, things like that?"

"Yeah." He dragged the word out, not sure of what was coming.

"Want to have an idol-smashing party in the parking lot?"

Now it was his turn to grin. "You kiddin' me? Those

ugly Hindu idols? You know I always hated those things. I'm in, man! Let me get my tools."

I got the box from the closet and carried it to the parking lot where he joined me, tools at the ready. The scent of sandalwood incense spilled out when I opened the box. We lined the idols up on the concrete lot and began beating the fire out of them. When we were done, they were unrecognizable. We gathered the pieces and tossed them into the garbage can. They were gone from my life for good.

God sent another dream that winter. In it I stood in a large room made of smooth, light-colored granite. Hindu symbols and other artifacts adorned the room. Set into the floor was an agni fire pit, used for sacrifices to the deities. Suddenly, a white, fiery light filled the place, driven by a strong wind. Though I was not hurt — I didn't even feel heat from the flame — everything in the room and the room itself were completely consumed.

I asked some of my Christian friends from church what they thought the dream meant.

"That was God burning up the leftover junk from your life as a Hindu," one man said. While I had been faithful to remove everything I could from my past in Hinduism, I needed God to finish the job.

During the summer of 1994, it hit me. I was still a member of the Hindu temple! As a Christ-follower, I needed to sever that connection, so I wrote them a letter explaining that I was no longer Hindu, that I believed in Jesus Christ.

INSIDE OUT

About a week after I mailed the letter — the time it would take it to arrive at the monastery on Kauai — I had an encounter.

I was sleeping soundly when something yanked me awake, wide-awake. It was the middle of the night. I sensed a presence in the room, and I recognized it. It looked like what I had worshipped in the monastery — the god Muruga. However, it was not the happy little god that I knew, or thought I knew. It looked angry. I was scared as I saw it start to hover over me, and I saw its face — Muruga, but twisted into something dark and malevolent. Demonic.

"No." My voice was little more than a whimper. "Leave me. I do not belong to you anymore."

Good. A little stronger. "Jesus Christ is my Lord and Savior now." The entity became more agitated.

I sat up. "In Jesus' name, leave." It left. I wanted someone to pray with, but I was alone. I had to do the praying.

Suddenly, God let me see how very wrong my idolatry was, how I had offended holy God by replacing him with idols made by human hands. My soul grieved at that. I fell, wholly broken, before God. I cried out to him, asking for his forgiveness. I could see how God was removing the shards of my former life, my life before Christ, piece by piece.

The next morning, I called the pastor.

"I knew this would happen," he said. "Come on in to my office right away."

He greeted me with his great mustached smile, warm handshake and a hug. "How you doing, brother?"

"That's more or less what I'm hoping you can tell me."

"Come right on in. Can I get you some coffee?"

"I don't drink coffee, but I could use a glass of water."

"Sure. Have a seat. I'll be right back with your water."

His office looked and smelled like a library. The walls were lined with books. I knew from previous visits he had them in a particular order.

He returned with the drinks and sat down at his desk. "Ah, got to have my coffee before we tackle this. Let's start out with prayer."

He asked God to be present and active in our meeting and to give us wisdom and guidance. It wasn't a long prayer, but it was earnest and passionate.

When he finished, he sat back and folded his hands on his desk.

"Now, brother, tell me your dream again. Try not to leave out any details."

The pastor was a thorough listener, seldom interrupting until the other person had told his or her entire story. He would tilt his head to the side, nodding his understanding from time to time and giving verbal cues that he was totally engrossed in what was being said. When I finished, he leaned forward and steepled his index fingers. Pressing them to his lips, he looked off to the side in thought.

Finally, he spoke. "Chinmoy, as believers in Jesus Christ, we're all in a spiritual war against the archenemy of

God. Call him Satan. Call him the devil. He attempts to get at God by attacking God's special creation, man." He went on to explain that while we live in this physical world, there is another realm that exists: the spiritual realm. What happens in it affects us as surely as what happens in the physical world we know.

He opened his Bible and read from the New Testament book of Ephesians. "For our struggle is not against flesh and blood, but against the rulers, against the authorities, against the powers of this dark world and against the spiritual forces of evil in the heavenly realms. Therefore put on the full armor of God, so that when the day of evil comes, you may be able to stand your ground, and after you have done everything, to stand" (Ephesians 6:12-13).

He talked to me about spiritual ties — idols, books, practices that could keep me spiritually bound. He laughed when I told him about getting my friend Derek to join in my idol-smashing party.

"I threw my books away and wrote a letter renouncing Hinduism and declaring myself a follower of Jesus Christ. I think I've covered all my bases." The pastor grinned and nodded at that.

Then he became serious again. "Chinmoy, there's one base you missed."

I shot him a questioning look.

"What about your name, Chinmoy Devananda?"

"I ... I'll need some time to think about that one."

"That's fine. Pray about it. Meanwhile, I have a book

I'd like you to read." He handed it to me. "Read it. Then we'll get together and discuss it."

Not long after that, I gave him a call.

"Hello, Pastor. This is Thomas. Or at least it will be, as soon as I can get my name legally changed back."

❧❧❧

I wish I could say, "And we all lived happily ever after." But as long as we're in these human bodies, we will sometimes suffer heartaches. Robin divorced me — I had no choice in the matter — after 19 years of marriage.

I took Bill's advice to attempt reconnection and reconciliation with my birth father. His addictions had broken him physically, mentally and financially. He had, of course, totally dissipated Aunt Millie's assets. Since I'd last seen him, he'd been in and out of treatment centers, jail and homeless shelters.

At one point, I told him about Jesus Christ, remembering those long conversations with Bill over garlic-cheese bread at The Cookie Cutter. Bill had presented the good news about God's only son in such a simple way that a young Hindu man could understand. I followed that example with my father.

I explained that we all are sinners, meaning every one of us breaks God's law and falls short of his holiness, his perfection.

"We all deserve God's judgment," I said. "But because he loves us so much, he sent his son, Jesus, to pay the price for our sin, to clear our record. Jesus, who had never sinned, was beaten and nailed to a cross, where he died to clear my name of so many sins. And yours, Dad, if you'll accept his payment.

"The best part of the story is he didn't stay dead. The Bible says that after three days in the tomb, he came back to life! He's a living God, not like the idols I worshiped when I was in the monastery.

"Our account is cleared when we first repent of our sin. Repentance means we hate our sin as much as God does and turn away from it. Then we need to accept Jesus' payment for us."

Dad prayed with me that summer day in 2012, becoming a follower of Christ. He died the following March.

That same month, I married Hannah, an amazing woman I met through an online Christian dating site. We have a blended family of five children, two of whom are in college.

In January 2014, I became manager of a store in Prineville, Oregon. It was hard to move because we had so many connections at our church there, so many dear friends. The pastor was my mentor and spiritual dad, second only to Bill. I still meet with him from time to time.

Often, when people move to a new town, it takes forever to find a church home, a place that is a comfortable fit. That was not the case with our move to Prineville. We visited Eastside Church, and that was it.

From the moment we walked in the door, we felt at home. Love, peace and compassion radiated from the people as they welcomed us. Senior Pastor Dusty and his wife, Twila, the women's pastor, invited us to lunch following the morning service that first Sunday. The church people even helped us move in and get settled. Eastside truly had a "family" feel.

Along the way, I became certain that God was calling me to preach. Hannah supported me in that calling. In fact, when we first became acquainted, she said she felt the Lord wanted her to be a pastor's wife. That was one thing that drew us together. I took a first step toward preparing for my own calling by agreeing to teach a men's Bible study at Eastside. I'd heard that the teacher always learns more than the students. I counted on that because I had much to learn. Work still required a huge chunk of my time, as I got things in order there, but I looked to the future when I could get my degree in pastoral studies.

My life came to reveal a picture of God's steadfast love. He pursued me to woo me to Christ. Bill called him "the Hound of Heaven." I liked that. I determined to forever praise him for hounding me.

"You shall have no other gods before me. You shall not make for yourself an image in the form of anything in heaven above or on the earth beneath or in the waters below." (Exodus 20:4)

LETTING GO
The Story of Melissa
Written by Audrey Jackson

The memory of the day Dad left stays with me like a bad song lyric, a chorus that keeps playing even when the radio is off. It was sunny but not warm. The fall breeze bit at my legs and kneecaps, barely covered by my navy knee socks. I crossed my arms and pulled my navy- and maroon-striped sweater closer around me as Hannah Morgan followed me off the bright yellow school bus and walked beside me down the sidewalk.

We were 5 and still getting used to walking home from school.

Approaching my house, I saw them. Dad's suitcases sat in the driveway in front of our 1968 Oregon ranch-style home. My feet were lead, forcing myself up two steps and standing beneath the covered sun porch.

Before I could turn the handle, Mom opened the door. Her eyes were heavy, and my baby sister Charlotte was wrapped in her arms. Charlotte was still in her pajamas.

"Mom, why is all this stuff in the driveway?" Her eyes averted mine.

"Your dad and sister Autumn are leaving today."

Anger and hurt swelled inside the deepest part of my gut. It was Mom's fault, surely. I grabbed Charlotte from my mother's arms and ran down the hallway to my room, holding my sister's baby belly with one thin arm. Her chubby legs swung as I ran. In my room, I laid Charlotte beside me on the quilted bed and let out a deep and debilitating cry.

Though it was my favorite, I never wore that sweater again.

༄ ༄ ༄

Hate's a funny thing. It's enticing and attractive. Hate makes you believe that if you pick it up and carry it on your back each day, that it will ease the loud aching of your beating heart. It's there every morning, tempting you to pick it up, and the longer you choose to carry it, the tighter and tighter it latches on. And while it didn't come naturally to me, I chose to strap it to my back, slump over and tread through life.

It would take many years for me to figure out that I didn't want to carry it.

༄ ༄ ༄

About two years after Dad left, Autumn came back to live with us in the old ranch house. He called about once a month, and when he did, all hell broke loose. I'd hear my parents arguing about child support, hearing only Mom's voice. It echoed against the walls and made her sound angry and shrill. She handed us the phone, our small childish hands pushing it against the sides of our faces.

"Hey, Dad!"

"Hey, Melbel."

"Dad, are you coming anytime soon?"

"Melissa, your mom makes it impossible to come and visit. She doesn't want me there. You hear how she talks to me."

I heard the convincing insistence in his voice, and it seemed reasonable. I decided that all of it — their divorce, his absence and his rejection — was Mom's fault. I was convinced that eventually she and my stepdad, Phil, would also abandon me. So, the older I got, I did everything in my power to test her. I'd lash out, yelling and disrespecting her for no reason.

"Where are you going, Melissa?"

"What do you care?"

"Melissa, be fair." Mom's throat grew tight, and her voice seemed tired.

"Just mind your own business, and stay out of mine." The door slammed behind me.

I became a person I didn't really like, but I did what I wanted and lived life in a way that made me feel as if I had control. I had always been taught that we are given free will, and I exercised my freedom to choose. I liked having the choice to do what I wanted with my body. I felt loose and free and wild. I drank and smoked and lied to my family about the things I was doing with my boyfriend in the backseat of his car.

I wasn't a mean-spirited kid, not at the heart of it. I went to a local church with my best friend, Ruby, every Tuesday and Sunday for seven years. The church hymnal felt familiar in my hands. I'd sit still and listen from the back row about how God was a God to be feared and respected. God, to me, was a serious thing. And while I believed in him, I didn't understand that he was anything more than the creator of the world and the giver of life.

Though at the time it felt important, solely believing in him didn't give me much. Church, though, was closely tied to my friendship with Ruby. We attended youth events, cookouts and services together for a good portion of our lives. She was, to me, what it looked like to be a Christian.

❧❧❧

High school graduation signaled official freedom. I was 17 years old when I fell in love with Joshua. He was 22, athletic and strong, and I liked the way his arms wrapped around me. It felt good to have someone want me. Despite Mom's displeasure, we moved in together a few months before I turned 18. Joshua instructed me to never talk about my God. He told me that he didn't believe that a god existed, and he asked that I not talk about it in his house. Because I wanted to make him happy, I listened. What I didn't realize at the time was that he had this way of controlling me. Though he only stood at 5 feet, 8 inches tall, he emotionally towered over me.

Joshua and I had only lived together a few months when Ruby came to our front door. I greeted her with a smile.

"Hey, Rubes, I wasn't expecting you."

"Hey, Melissa. Yeah, I figured I'd stop by for a bit. Is Josh around?"

"No, just me. Why?" I looked at her curiously.

"Well, there's something that's been really pressing on me. I was curious if we could chat."

I sat down. "Sure, what's up?"

"I just don't think you're living the way that you need to be. And I don't think you should be living with Joshua. I don't think it's good for you. As your friend and as someone who really believes in what the Bible says about right and wrong, I just don't think I can support you any longer. I don't think we can be friends the way that we always have."

My heart was crushed. My head felt heavy, and anger began filling me. Someone else had walked out on me.

And if Ruby could no longer face me, I was positive God couldn't, either.

᷂᷂᷂᷂

The bell on the door of the drugstore chimed loudly as I exited. A nervous feeling filled my stomach, and I wished to draw no attention to myself. I tucked my purchased pregnancy tests beneath my arm and drove back to the home Joshua and I had purchased nearby.

I had been too afraid to even mention my suspicion to my husband. We had been married for three years, and though I had always wanted children, Joshua refused. He had no interest in being a father.

I took the test three times. Sitting on the toilet in the bathroom in a fit of fear, I picked up the phone and dialed the number of my friend Lisa. Lisa was pregnant with her first child, and we had often talked about how incredible it would be to be mothers. Her hello was cheerful and encouraging.

"Lisa, I think I'm pregnant."

"Oh, Melissa! So … what are you going to do?" She knew Joshua's stance on children.

"Well, I guess I'm going to tell Josh."

"Good luck. Let me know how it goes."

The day felt as if it contained a dozen extra hours. Joshua was working the graveyard shift that night for a local manufacturer. He wouldn't be home until late into the night. The sun had long disappeared when I scribbled a message onto a pink Post-it note and stuck it to the front of the living room television set.

Please wake me up when you get home. We need to talk about something.

The sun was still hidden beneath a quilt of dark sky when I felt someone shaking my shoulder. I recognized Joshua's rough hands and the smell of the industrial glue streaked across his blue jeans.

"What?" he muttered apathetically.

My eyes took a moment to adjust to being open. I sat up against the bed's backboard and hugged the covers close.

I began to recognize his navy blue shirt, snug against his athletic frame. His reddish-blond, coarse hair was dirty from where his hands had brushed it away from his forehead. Quick and impatient, he repeated himself.

"What?"

"I … I think I'm pregnant." Large tears slowly rolled down my cheeks, flushed from nervousness. My hands trembled, clutching the soft comforter closer to my pajamas.

"Are you sure?" He conveyed a tone of agitation.

"I took three pregnancy tests."

His back turning toward me, his muscular shoulders faced me.

"I won't believe you until you get a note from your doctor."

And as he walked away, I muttered a weak, "Okay."

తతతత

Joshua's words whipped and stung. He lashed out harshly, never forgiving me for getting pregnant. Never letting me forget that he was better than me. Smarter than me. I was nothing. Though he hit me, I was most affected by his harsh and unfeeling remarks. His attitude beat me down, day by day. Joshua reopened the childhood wounds I'd worked so hard to stitch closed.

Finally, when our daughter Lexi was 5 years old, I asked Joshua to leave. It was a day in April, and somehow I felt the promise of a new beginning. It was a hard decision.

Mom was hospitalized and treated for a form of

leukemia. A few months later, she left us with an empty hospital bed and a searing heartache.

The day after Mom died, I decided to call Dad and invite him to Mom's funeral. My father was living in Bend, Oregon, but I hadn't spoken to him in a few months. He had been married several more times since he had left us as children, and I hadn't had any desire to see him.

The telephone rang in my ear, then Dad's deep voice sounded on the other end. "Hello?"

"Hi, Dad."

"Oh, hey, Melbel. What's going on?" My muscles tensed up. I was working two jobs and trying to support my daughter alone. I felt the weight of exhaustion against my shoulders, and it pushed them downward, slumping me forward and over the edge of the cushioned chair.

"Well, Dad, I'm calling to see if you'll come to Mom's funeral. I'd really like you to be there."

His voice became curt, as if he was offended I'd even suggested it.

"I'm *not* coming."

"What?" I said, surprised.

"I'm not coming to your mother's funeral. I think she got exactly what she deserved." My jaw dropped as I listened to my father's cutting words.

"What does that mean?"

"I'm not coming to the funeral."

"Okay," I said, hanging up the phone. I leaned back against the chair. And as I shut my eyes, the hate in my heart grew so very black that it was almost unrecognizable.

LETTING GO

And soon, I began trying to douse my anger and hatred with alcohol, which only ended up causing it to flame and burn like wildfire.

<p style="text-align:center">~~~</p>

The beeping sound of my old white Honda reminded me to buckle my seatbelt as 15-year-old Lexi slid onto the seat beside me and shut the passenger door. She glanced out the passenger side window, and the golden light of the afternoon sun made her hair shine five different shades of blond. I couldn't help but think about how beautiful she was and how the years had passed so quickly.

I put the car in drive and headed into town toward Eastside Church where Lexi had been attending youth group for a few years. When she turned 8, I'd decided that she ought to be able to make an informed decision about whether God existed and whether or not a belief in God was something she wanted for her life. She'd become enthralled and overjoyed with the idea of having a relationship with God.

She glanced over at me.

"Mom, you should come to church with me tonight. You don't even have to go to big church. You could come with me to youth and sit with your friend Sarah. She's a youth leader, remember?" She put inflection upon the word remember and smiled, giving me a bit of her spunky sass. I could feel the heat move from my toes to my ears, anger and offense coursing through me.

INSIDE OUT

"Lexi, just because I don't go to church doesn't mean I don't believe in God." Keeping my eyes on the road, I pointed my finger at her. She backed into the right side of the car seat, and her hazel eyes grew large and round.

"You don't know if I talk to God or not, and don't make me feel like I'm a bad person because I choose not to go to church. We aren't discussing this anymore."

Lexi grew quiet and recognized that I wasn't interested in arguing. I dropped her off, said goodbye and sat in the parking lot with a book until it was time to pick her up. I wanted my daughter to know God, but I was positive that God didn't want to know me. Not after all of the poor decisions I'd made. Not after my heart had turned black and hard.

Eight p.m. rolled around, and I pulled to the curb where Lexi stood with her friends. Rolling down the window, I hollered her name. Her mouth formed into a large grin as she waved goodbye to the other high school students and hopped in the car. The sky was still holding on to some red summer light.

"How was church?" I asked, pretending like our earlier conversation hadn't taken place.

"It was good." She paused for a good 10 seconds and then grinned. "But I really wish you'd come with me."

Lexi's insistence eventually proved successful, and she convinced me to visit Sunday service with her. I had no intention of enjoying it. In fact, the only thing I had on my mind was eating breakfast at a local restaurant afterward. I persuaded my boyfriend at the time, Matt, to come with

84

us, and he brought his daughter Mary with him. Approaching the front door, I glanced at my reflection. I made sure that my makeup and hair were impeccable, and I had even added a dainty necklace to my outfit.

Walking into the large foyer, I recognized several extended family members. I veered away from them, embarrassed to be standing in a church building for the first time since high school. A stranger greeted me, and I immediately glanced around at Matt and Mary. Did they also think it was odd for a stranger to be saying hello to us?

We sat in the second to the last row, near the exit, and my hand brushed the side of Matt's faded jeans as we scooted down to our seats. In front of us, on the wall, hung a large cross. When the music started, I felt like I had suddenly been teleported to a concert. The music was joyful and exciting. It was an atmosphere I'd never experienced in all seven years of attending church as a girl. I noticed that the people in front of me began raising their hands. Something seemed different.

"Lexi," I whispered. "What kind of church is this again?"

"Mom, just sing." She grinned.

The air got heavy, and I felt the need to concentrate on the song lyrics up on the screen. We sang about how Jesus died for us. The air became too thick. Too heavy. Sitting down, I began to sob. Overwrought with embarrassment and not comprehending what was causing me to cry, I buried my head in my lap. Mascara ran down my face, clumping and sticking on my cheeks. And yet a sense of peace permeated every part of me. I felt like something had broken down the thin wall of hate I'd put up between myself and the rest of the world.

God somehow seemed more approachable in that tan- and rust-colored sanctuary, and I thought that just maybe I'd like to know him.

❧❧❧

My daughter was overjoyed when I began attending church with her on Wednesday nights. I was, too, really. It was all so new and exciting. My life, however, was still heavy with the feelings of rejection and abandonment. I carried them around like weights around my legs and arms. Only, instead of building strength and muscle, they drained me of life and energy. I heard, really heard, for the first time a message of forgiveness. Forgiveness, though, was for people who deserved it. I wasn't one of those people, and I was sure that the boyfriends of my past, my ex-husband and my parents did not deserve forgiveness. I had not deserved the hand life had dealt me, and those individuals did not deserve a pardon.

So, I strapped hate and bitterness on tighter and tighter. And, though I was open to the idea of attending church, I was still reluctant to be around other church-attending adults. I felt sure they were all better and more worthy than me.

It wasn't very crowded the night I met Ian. He stood in

front of me in the church dinner line, and I saw him looking at me as he ladled out his soup.

"Hey, there, what's your name again?"

"Hi, I'm Melissa." I stuck out my hand.

"Why don't you sit with me, Melissa? I'd like to get to know you better."

"Okay, sure." I could think of no reason not to. I normally sat with Lexi and her friends. Sitting with adults would be a nice change.

"So, Melissa, how long have you been attending Eastside?"

"Oh, only a few months now. I have a daughter Lexi who attends the youth group. I normally come and go to youth with her on Wednesday nights." I took a sip of my soda. I realized I had met Ian's wife when I was younger. Conversation came easy, and he made me feel comfortable.

"Hey, Mom. Are you ready to go to the youth room?" Lexi came over and put her arm around the back of my chair.

"You know, hon, I think I'm going to go to big people church tonight." Her eyes grew large and bright, shining in disbelief.

"You are, huh? Well, have fun with that."

She walked off, and Ian and I cleared our table and headed into the auditorium. The church was very slowly beginning to fill up, and I noticed Ian settle down on the sixth row of seats. It was a large contrast to my back row Sunday morning seat, but I slid in the row behind him. I scooted down a bit so that I could see over his head during the sermon.

Toward the end of the set of praise songs, I noticed Ian sitting very still in his seat. His arm rested on the back of the chair beside him, and he appeared to be in a serious state of concentration. The last song began playing, and in a sudden, powerful realization, I was overcome by the knowledge that I needed God to change my life. I needed his forgiveness. I could feel my heart being moved. And after years and years of shutting people out and protecting myself from getting hurt, I craved the peace and love that came with knowing a heavenly father existed who would never leave. Even in my worst moments. He would never leave.

My shoulders heaved up and down the way a ship rocks on choppy water.

Pastor Dusty walked out onto the floor, level with our seats.

"I feel as if there is someone here tonight who feels lost. You've been holding tightly to your own strength but are ready to recommit your life to God."

My tears grew into louder sobs, and I felt Ian's hand gently press against mine. His voice was soft, almost a whisper. But I could hear him loud and clear.

"You know this is for you, right?"

"You think so?" Mascara ran down to the tip of my nose, and I was reminded of the last time I had cried in church, several months before. He peered across at me, smile lines framing the corners of his eyes.

"Melissa, there's no doubt in my mind." He paused, looking down. His eyes then returned to me. "You know, I never sit this far back, but tonight I felt God telling me to stop right here. I feel I'm here to pray with you, if you'd like."

"Absolutely."

And in that moment, I began to let go. I began to slowly lay down the heavy loads of hatred, regret and broken relationships I had carried for so very many years.

❧❧❧

I let out a deep breath as I walked out of the sanctuary and into the church lobby. I was slowly beginning to feel comfortable coming to services each Sunday. The people were so genuine and kind. I knew I was where I needed to be. Making my way toward the door, I heard a familiar voice.

"Melissa! Hey, come here a second." Ian motioned me over to a table by the wall. "Are you signing up for Restorations class?"

"Well, what is it?" I asked, Ian steering me over to the signup table.

"The class is all about healing past hurting and rebuilding and restoring our soul. You learn key tools to handle the enemy and learn all about forgiveness. You know, how to give forgiveness, receive it and walk right with the Lord."

"Well, it sounds like a good thing. Sure, I'll sign up."

Though it was hard to admit, I knew there was so much I held onto that I needed to forget and forgive. I was hesitant to begin the class, but it was one of the best decisions I've ever made. It pushed me to let go of so many pent-up hurts and wounds. It was a 16-week commitment, and each week I could feel God challenging me in new and uncomfortable ways. At the beginning of the class, they instructed us to write a letter to God, handing over all the areas of our life that we wanted God to take from us. Over the course of five weeks, sitting in the chair and surrounded by several other people, I wrote five long letters. There was so much to let go of.

Over and over, I would hand areas of my life over to God, and then without realizing it, I would pick them up and clutch onto them. Each time, I'd intentionally write another letter to God. I wanted more than anything to give him every part of my hurting heart, despite the fact that it was often so difficult.

I found, though, that with each passing week, God was showing me how to let go of hurts. He was showing me how to accept his forgiveness and extend it to other people. By the end of the class, I recognized all the many ways God was releasing me from my burdens. There was one burden, though, I thought would never leave. A wound that would never be healed. I often thought of my father, and I wondered if he ever thought about me.

❧❧❧

Christmas was a few weeks away when my sister Autumn sent me a text, asking me to bring Lexi to a Christmas celebration on December 28.

"Of course!" I texted her back, excitedly.

"Great. There will be about nine of us. Can't wait to see you."

I walked into my bathroom to shower and get ready for work. My day-to-day life had become so much easier, and I found that even waking up was full of so much more peace and purpose than when I had lived begrudgingly, holding on to my hurts and mistakes. Turning on the shower faucet, I reflected on the conversation I had with my friend Sandra the previous Sunday.

"Melissa, do you think you'll ever be able to repair your relationship with your dad?" I had stood next to her in the church auditorium, leaning against the chair in front of me.

"You know, Sandra, I really don't. I don't even know where he's living now. We haven't spoken in nearly eight years. I just wonder if that's a burden I'll always carry."

"I'm going to be praying about that, Mel. I believe God can do things we never expect."

My mind became alert to the running water as I stepped into the shower. The water ran down all around me, and I seized in a sudden panic. Water spilled into my mouth as I spoke aloud. "Nine people. That must mean Dad and his wife will be there." I stood there, melting in the sudden comprehension and fear of seeing my father. But then, in a moment of peace, I felt that just perhaps

Sandra had been right. I was getting stronger as a woman of God, and perhaps he had specifically arranged the reunion. I suddenly realized that everything would be okay.

On a snowy and cold day, Lexi and I loaded up our truck and drove to the Christmas celebration. The drive up to my sister's mountain home was unbearable. My hands trembled as they clutched the steering wheel, and I pulled into the driveway in front of her beautiful, natural wood home. My mind raced the way a toy car races around a track, quick and loud. *What if he yelled at me? What would it be like to see him? Could I truly and fully forgive him and myself for years of pent-up anger?*

I didn't recognize one of the cars, and my heart beat like a drum as we walked up the stairs and into my sister's home. Lexi looked over at me and whispered, "Are you okay?" I nodded, and we walked up the stairs.

Lexi and I set our purses down on the living room floor as my sister came over and gave me a hug. Everyone was congregated in the kitchen, and we migrated toward it, the floor feeling like the ocean and my feet like weighty anchors. Dad and his wife, Milly, stood together, and Milly flashed me a sincere-looking smile.

"Hi," I said. The room seemed to pulse with a million silent conversations.

Dad stared at me with his twinkling blue eyes. They reminded me of sapphires. Blue and piercing in the light. He stood there uncomfortably, and I noticed his black Irish hair was salted with gray.

"Hi," he replied.

"Well, I guess I'll be the first. Give me a hug." Milly crossed the kitchen and drew me close. She was warm, and I could see Dad looking at me from behind her. She let go of me and moved over to hug Lexi. I looked over at Dad, and in a rush of sudden courage that could only have come from God, I walked over and wrapped my arms around his waist. I squeezed him with purpose and resolution, and a wave of tension released from my muscles as I felt him slip his arms around me. For the first time in eight years, I was hugging my father. My tears fell onto the collar of his shirt, and my back shook with crying against his hand. He also began to cry, and I felt him relax beside me.

The walls between us crumbled, and all was forgotten.

It was time to begin again.

కకకక

It is difficult to believe that I once was so distant from a father who is now so involved in the life of my daughter and me. Sometimes, I look at his twinkling eyes, and I am reminded of just how much can change when you choose to let the change happen. My restored relationship with Dad is forever my reminder that God changes hearts.

God removed from me a heart enveloped with layers of hate and unforgiveness and gave me life. He showed me how to let go. He showed me how to love. More than anything, he showed me I am worthy of being loved and forgiven.

INSIDE OUT

∽∽∽

From Restorations

Forgiveness is a decision I make to obey God and to walk in a lifestyle in a higher realm, by not allowing someone else's actions or attitudes to dictate my actions or attitudes, releasing them from harm to God, while not requiring them to be accountable to me to make it right, with a willingness to move in the opposite spirit, making sure I am willing for God to use me as an unrestricted channel of his love to that person.

Forgiveness is not:

1. Forgiveness is not a feeling.
2. Forgiveness is not saying you were not hurt.
3. Forgiveness is not saying the people who hurt you were not wrong.
4. Forgiveness is not necessarily being able to trust that person again.
5. Forgiveness is not alleviating responsibility from anyone.

If you are struggling with forgiveness or seeking to overcome past hurt, we welcome you to attend Eastside Church's Restorations class offered each fall and winter. Find out class times and sign up at www.eastsidefoursquare.org under "Connect" and "Classes/Studies."

CHOOSE THE WONDERFUL
The Story of Jessica
Written by Lisa Bradshaw

"Please, Mom, I don't want to go," I begged.

"Don't be silly, Jessica. It's your turn to feed the dogs," my mom insisted.

"But I don't want to go with Dad. I want to stay here with you."

"That's enough, Jessica. You have chores to do," my dad ordered as he spanked me and moved me in the direction of the door. "Let's go."

The shop where we kept the hunting dogs was about a mile from the house. As we drove to the shop, I held back tears and tried not to think about what was coming. I tried holding out hope that maybe this time he wouldn't touch me or make me touch him, but I knew better. Feeding the dogs almost always meant I would have to do something that made my stomach ache and my heart race with fear.

An hour later, we returned to the house just after dusk. I quietly tiptoed into the bathroom, then shut the door and locked it behind me. Careful to avoid the hole in the floor between the bathtub and the toilet, I grabbed the towel hanging over the curtain rod. I closed the toilet seat and sat down, covering my face with the towel so no one could hear me cry.

Just then, a cockroach scurried across my feet, so I

quickly brought my knees to my chest and wrapped my arms around my legs, holding my feet up off the floor. Our old house was built on cement blocks without a proper foundation, and the hole in the bathroom floor made it easy for bugs to enter and exit at their leisure. As much as I feared the bugs I knew were lurking about, nothing scared me more than my own dad.

"Jessica, you get to bed now," my dad whispered through the locked door.

I didn't answer him.

"I mean it," he said, sharpening his tone. "Now."

"Okay," I whispered through the towel still muffling my tears.

I did as he said and went straight to bed. I closed my eyes tight and tried not to think about what had happened and waited for sleep to come. By morning, I would be in my safe place again.

కాకాకా

It had been three years since we moved away from our extended family. We had only moved from Northern Louisiana to Southern Louisiana, but it was far enough away that we were isolated from everyone outside our immediate family. We had moved when my dad bought some property to farm, but we were still poor.

I was lonely without my PawPaw. He was my dad's dad, but he was nothing like my dad. He was kind and funny and used to make me feel protected when he was near. He came to visit us frequently after we moved and eventually moved about 30 minutes from us.

"I love you, PawPaw." I would cheer with glee as I flew through the sky while riding on his shoulders. He was 6 feet, 8 inches tall and was a tower of safety when I was with him.

"Hold on tight," he would say as he ran through the yard. He made me feel like I could fly.

PawPaw rarely spent time at our home. He would usually pick us kids up and take us back to his house for our visits, so I don't think he knew the extent of the damage his son was causing our family. He never saw the beatings my brothers and I endured or the way he slapped my mom around, and he definitely never saw my dad's hands on me in a sexual way.

"If you don't do it, then we won't go to the circus this weekend," my dad would threaten me. "You don't want to ruin everyone's trip to the circus, do you? Your brothers will hate you for it."

I didn't care about the circus, but I didn't want my brothers to be mad at me. I knew my dad would make something up that I had done to get in trouble as the reason we couldn't go, then my brothers would blame me for spoiling it for all of us.

"I bought you something today," my dad would say as he handed me a locket or a necklace or a mood ring. "If you keep our secret, you can have it."

I didn't want to keep our secret, but I was afraid to tell anyone. I felt all alone, like I couldn't count on anyone to save me from him. Thankfully, I did have one safe place to go.

❧❧❧

"Good morning, Jessica." Mrs. Bradley greeted me as I walked into school. Her classroom was filled with colorful letters from the alphabet and the smell of dried paint from the previous day's project. From our learning stations to our book corner, Mrs. Bradley's classroom cheered mightily: "Come inside. It's fun to learn!"

"Good morning, Mrs. Bradley," I replied, giving her a big hug as I entered my kindergarten classroom.

Each child who entered Mrs. Bradley's classroom was greeted with the same warm welcome. Just hearing her voice brought me peace.

"Okay, class. Today is Friday, so we know what that means. We have a special visitor today," she said as she gently wiggled her hand inside our class puppet. "Can everyone say, 'Good morning, Mr. Peabody'?"

"Good morning, Mr. Peabody," we squealed in unison.

For eight hours a day, I was free of my dad. I was a lonely and frightened girl at home, and Mrs. Bradley's classroom was the only place I felt safe. She opened up a world of possibility to me, and best of all, I knew he couldn't hurt me when I was there.

❧❧❧

Summers were the worst time of year because I couldn't go to school. I had to be home more than usual and was forced to succumb to my dad's desires when he pressed them upon me. It didn't just happen when feeding the dogs, and it didn't happen every day, but it happened whenever he wanted me, and going to school was the only way for me to get away from him.

By summer's end, I couldn't wait to go back to school and meet my new teacher.

"Come in, and sit down," Ms. Anderson curtly said as I walked into her classroom. I immediately felt an ache in my stomach as I looked around the room.

It didn't feel as inviting as Mrs. Bradley's, and it wasn't as colorful. It wouldn't take long for me to figure out that my new teacher, Ms. Anderson, also wasn't as inviting or colorful, and she made up her mind about me right away.

"You're going to be just like your cousins," Ms. Anderson accused. "Just poor white trash."

My cousins lived nearby in filthy conditions. They had mice and pet feces inside their house and often suffered open sores on their skin from scratching flea bites. They were always in trouble at school and showed little respect for their elders, but I wasn't like them.

I loved school because I wanted to learn. I wanted to make friends and be surrounded by people who cared about me and helped me succeed. I loved school because it was my safe place.

But she didn't seem to understand all that. In no time at all, my safe place turned into a series of daily struggles.

INSIDE OUT

"Can I have a snack, please?" I asked Ms. Anderson as she passed crackers and juice out to the rest of the class.

"No," she snapped. "You're already fat and getting fatter. You don't need a snack."

Some of the kids laughed at me and made fun of me when I started gaining weight during first grade, but I kept eating and hiding behind the food, trying to fill a hole inside of me that couldn't be filled.

🙟🙟🙟

Things at home got even worse after my dad's grandma died. His own mom had been a horribly mean woman, so he had sought solace in his grandmother when growing up. When she died, he became bitter and forced our family to suffer along with him.

"Don't you dare tell your mother," my dad threatened as he buttoned up his pants. "I'll kill her if you do."

No longer was he buying me jewelry to keep me quiet or threatening to take the circus away. Now he was threatening to kill my mom and sometimes my brothers and me, too. He was violent and dangerous, and I knew he was capable of killing us all.

"If you tell anyone, I'll go to prison," he warned me, pointing his finger in my face. "I'll offer you to my friends, and you'll wish it was back to just you and me."

He walked out of the shop, still tucking his shirt into his pants, and the door slammed behind him. I waited until I was sure he was gone and then snuck back to the house and into my bedroom. I picked up my teddy bear and lay on my bed, clutching him in my arms as I sobbed. When I could no longer take the pounding in my head from crying so hard and for so long, I sat up on the edge of the bed and held Teddy on my lap facing me.

My dad's not going to make me cry anymore.

I'm putting you away and will never cry to you about my dad again.

I'd grown exhausted by the torrent of tears my dad caused me over and over. Most of all, I'd grown tired of feeling like my dad controlled me, and I couldn't break free.

"No more," I proclaimed, as I wiped the tears from my face and set Teddy on top of my nightstand. "No more tears for him."

I made up my mind that it was the last time I would ever cry because of my dad and what he was doing to me. And it would be the last time I would seek comfort from my teddy bear. I was done crying and letting my dad win.

గొలిచిలి

When I was 10 years old, I went to a youth conference with my oldest brother, Donnie. He was invited by one of his coaches from school, so I tagged along. I hadn't been to church much unless I went with PawPaw, but I had gone occasionally.

I listened to the youth leader invite us to come forward and accept Jesus that day, and I thought about one of the first times my dad put his hands on me and made me put my hands on him. I remember I had wrapped myself in a ball when he was done.

"Now, you did this, too," he assured me. "You wanted this to happen, and it did."

When he left the room, I sobbed because I knew he wasn't right. I had told him "stop" over and over again, and I knew I didn't want to do what we were doing, but that was his way of convincing me that what we were doing was my fault, too.

God will never want me.

It's all my fault.

God can't love me anymore.

When the worship leader invited people to come forward if they needed to pray or wanted to know Jesus, it was the first time I felt a pull toward God since my dad started telling me that the things he made me do were my fault. Still, I hesitated.

I can't go up there.

God doesn't want me.

He'll reject me.

I told myself over and over again to ignore the tugging of God on my heart because God wouldn't want me once I got up there to pray.

I'll take off my shoes.

I can't go forward and pray with bare feet.

That would be inappropriate.

You're definitely supposed to have your shoes on in church, right?

I tried to ignore the way I felt by taking off my shoes. I knew I wouldn't go forward without my shoes and felt safe from risking being rejected by God.

No matter what prayers were said or what words were shared with me that day, I just couldn't bear the idea of God turning me away, so I turned him away instead.

ತ್ಗೊತ್ಗೊತ್ಗೊ

We went from living in a house with a hole in the bathroom floor to building a big, beautiful home when we sold some of our land and its profitable mineral rights.

During that time, segregation was causing volatile conflicts on the campuses of schools in the South, so my parents put us in private school. It seemed overnight we could afford anything we wanted. Part of me had hoped the relief of money stress would at least slow down the beatings of my mom and brothers, but we still couldn't figure out his triggers. We had no idea how to avoid them. One day he was fine with me riding my three-wheeler on trails near our house, but the next time he'd yell at me and tell me it was dangerous. Most of the time, he didn't care if I rode my bicycle on the street, but sometimes he might freak out and get furious with me for not riding on the side of the street.

"Jessica!" my dad shouted as he ran toward me. "Get off of there right now!"

I had been waiting for the bus for school and was walking along one of the tracks of the railroad, trying to keep my balance.

Surrounded by my friends and even a couple of their parents who waited with us for the bus most mornings, my dad charged toward me as he ripped his belt from his pants.

"What did I do? What did I do?" I cried, trying to stop him before he reached me with such rage.

There was no stopping him. In one powerful motion, he dragged me from the railroad tracks and started beating me with his belt.

"You stupid idiot!" he screamed. "You could've killed yourself!"

Over and over again, his belt slapped against me. My skirt didn't cover my lower legs, so each slap of his belt broke my skin and made me bleed.

"Don't ever do that again," he commanded as he let go of me and started looping his belt back through his pants. "Now straighten yourself up, and get in line for the bus."

I was humiliated everyone saw me get a beating, but I had to go to school, anyway. When I got to school, I cleaned myself up in the bathroom and tried to forget about what he did and who saw it happen.

❧❧❧

Money hadn't solved our family's problems, and eating more and more food hadn't solved mine, so when I started going to private school in sixth grade, I made up my mind to lose weight — a lot of weight. I was tired of being picked on and wanted to attract positive attention from someone other than my dad. By then, I had given up weighing myself when I reached 220 pounds and wore a women's size 22.

During that time, I met my friend Denise. She and her family ate healthy foods and exercised, so I was motivated to get the weight off after spending so much time at their house. I didn't know how to lose weight properly, so I cut my calories to no more than 300 calories per day and exercised up to four hours a day.

The weight started melting off, so I didn't care that I was having blackouts and headaches from starving myself.

My mom always told all of us kids that we could pretty much do whatever we wanted when it came to drugs, alcohol and sex — as long as we didn't lie about it — so I started testing the waters. I replaced food with whatever alcohol was around the house, like homemade wine that my mom let us drink because she didn't think it had enough alcohol in it to matter. As time went on, I got a little bolder and took sips of my dad's beer in front of him or charged a pack of cigarettes to his account at the convenience store. These choices made me feel more in control of my life, and the more control I felt I had, the less tolerance I had for what my dad was still doing to me.

I grew more and more angry at my dad for the things he'd forced me to do for so many years. Being around Denise and her family made me want to be more like them. I wanted to be normal, and I knew my dad was never going to stop forcing himself on me unless I made him. Each time he forced himself on me, I became more determined to make him stop but didn't know how. My rage built, and so did my willingness to fight him off — no matter what.

"Come on," he said as he tried touching me.

"No. You need to stop," I said firmly.

"Don't fight me."

"Leave me alone. Please, just leave me alone!" I pleaded.

"Come on. Stop fighting me."

"No! Leave me alone!" I screamed as I ran through the empty house and grabbed a butcher knife from the kitchen.

"What are you doing?" my dad yelled, shocked by my boldness.

"Don't ever touch me again," I warned him, my heart pounding as I held up the knife, angry and trying to be brave. "I'm going to keep this in my room, and if you ever try anything again, I will cut off everything that matters to you."

My dad didn't move a muscle.

"I mean it. Never again."

It was the last time my dad ever tried to touch me, and it was the first time I felt like anger overtook my fear. I was 13.

෧෧෧෧

I started eighth grade weighing 125 pounds and wearing a size 7. I drank a lot on the weekends with my friends and knew that the alcohol intake far exceeded my rule of no more than 300 calories per day. My solution for that was to take laxatives and diets pills, and if I consumed anything more than pickles and Diet Coke, including alcohol, I threw it up.

"Jessica!" Donnie yelled at me as he shook my shoulders. "Jessica, wake up."

When 125 pounds wasn't skinny enough for me, I pushed my weight loss even further and eventually weighed less than 115 pounds. That's when the fainting spells started.

"Wake up!"

I'd been standing in the kitchen making myself a salad when I blacked out in front of him. I slowly regained consciousness and almost wished I hadn't.

"What are you doing to yourself? I'm not going to watch you die," Donnie scolded as he helped me to the kitchen chair. "Enough with these salads. Your bones are sticking out."

"I know," I cried. "I know. I'm sorry."

Donnie had tried talking to me many times before, but I wouldn't listen to him. He'd been the only person to notice I was hurting myself by the way I chose to lose weight. He actually cared about what was happening to me, so I started making small changes to get better by adding dressing to my salad, eating a couple hundred more calories at a time and exercising only an hour a day instead of three to four hours. On the weekends, I still struggled with the guilt of consuming too many calories when drinking, so I would binge on alcohol and food, then throw up. I figured it was an improvement.

Slowly, I reached a more healthy weight, my eyes weren't sunken with dark circles and sitting in a chair got more comfortable since my bones no longer protruded from my back and buttocks.

The anger that crept in the night I threatened my dad with a knife remained with me. I became difficult to get along with at home and had little tolerance for my dad's presence. I obsessed about ways to kill myself. I even cut my wrists once but became terrified when I drew blood, so I stopped. Later, when my depression deepened, I tried again by overdosing on a combination of Benadryl and beer. It did nothing but make me sleep for 24 hours. I also started hitting myself, leaving small bruises. Nothing eased my desire to die and end the suffering, until the night I almost killed myself by accident.

I was only 15, which was the legal driving age in Louisiana, and I was driving our family Bronco toward town on a road with 5-foot-wide ditches on either side. I lived in a small town with only one convenience store off the main highway. I got used to crossing the railroad tracks to get to the main road through town, but the lights usually blinked yellow. This time, my mind was wandering again, wondering about ways I could kill myself, and I'd picked up speed, reaching 85 miles per hour. By the time I noticed the lights that were usually yellow were blinking red, it was too late to stop. I slammed on my brakes and slowed to 60, and the Bronco jumped the railroad tracks as a train sped by and barely missed the back of the car. I was propelled across the main street through town and barely missed an oncoming motorcycle.

I parked on the side of the road and tried to collect myself. It felt like I had been in a trance.

How did I not notice the blinking red lights?

Why didn't I slow down as I approached town instead of speeding up?

The close call on the railroad tracks helped me to see that maybe I didn't want to kill myself at all. Otherwise, I wouldn't have hit the brakes. I couldn't make sense of what had happened, but I no longer actively tried killing myself.

❧❧❧

I became good friends with a girl named Noelle in ninth grade, and her parents, Janice and Bill, were opening a restaurant in Baton Rouge that summer, so they asked me to move with them and work there until school started again in the fall. My parents were busy putting together a hunting camp and weren't paying much attention to what I was doing, so I agreed to go with Noelle's family to Baton Rouge.

Noelle's mom, Janice, made us go to church every Sunday. I only went because Janice told us to go, and she was taking good care of me, so I wanted to please her.

Strangely, when I went back home, my dad was around the house more — everyone was. Everyone but me carried on like we were a happy family and none of the dysfunction had ever taken place.

It made me furious. I couldn't stand it, so when Janice told me they were opening another restaurant in Tampa, Florida, and invited me to come with them, I jumped at the chance.

"Mom, I have decided to move to Tampa with Noelle's family and work at their new restaurant," I told her. I wasn't asking permission.

"Are you sure this is what you want?" she asked.

"I want to get out of here," I answered. "Dad sexually abused me and made me do things I never, ever wanted to do. He made me think it was all my fault and that I had wanted to do it."

My mom immediately began crying.

"I can't be here and act like we are one big happy family," I informed her. "I'm leaving."

"I wish I had known. I would've stopped it!" my mom cried.

My mom hugged me, telling me over and over how sorry she was that my dad had hurt me and that she didn't know about it.

I loved my mom, and I didn't blame her. For years, our family had been in survival mode. He hadn't touched me since my threat with the knife, and he had given up his abusive battle against us as well. My dad had stopped beating my brothers and me after Donnie beat him up. That was the last time he tried to hurt us. Donnie was as big as our dad by now, so there was no longer anything

Dad could get away with in our house, except the verbal cruelty he still shouted at us.

"It's just time for me to go."

৵৵৵৵

I moved to Tampa and got busy opening the new restaurant.

Mom decided to divorce Dad, and within three months, my mom and two younger brothers moved to Tampa. Janice hired her on at the restaurant and gave her a place to stay. Donnie stayed behind to live with his girlfriend's family, so he could finish his senior year of high school.

With 12 people living in one home, I lacked the privacy to binge and purge. And after Janice explained to me the long-term consequences of bulimia, I finally quit.

Around 2 a.m. one night, sirens began blaring, warning us of a hurricane on its way, so we loaded up what we could in Bill's truck and headed inland to a local college designated for evacuees. We had to spend a few days at the college until the storm passed and we were allowed to return home.

The Maranatha Christian Group for college outreach was having a worship service at the college, so we told Janice about it, thinking she would like the group and knowing she hadn't found a church home yet in Tampa. Watching Janice raise her hands in prayer and sing aloud with the praise music, I knew she'd missed church and would be looking for a church home for all of us again.

After the service, she met the leaders of the group who invited us to attend their church. We knew Janice would say yes. I didn't mind going along, either, as long as it meant Noelle and I could hang out with college guys.

Eventually, over time and one by one, my mom and little brothers, Bill and our friend Julie all committed their lives to God during different church services. They each made the decision to ask God to forgive them of the things they'd done wrong in their lives. They wanted to make life changes. I, however, didn't go forward.

Deep down, I was still afraid that God could never accept me after the things I had done with my dad. Even though I put a stop to it when I was 13, I still felt guilty for it ever happening at all.

"Jessica, God has a place for you. God has a place for all of us," Janice explained, determined to break through to me. She loved me like a daughter, even welcoming my mom and little brothers into her life. She had given us all a fresh start.

I wouldn't look at her and tried to resist what she told me. The same rage I felt when I threatened my dad with a knife returned. For a long time, I thought the anger building up inside over the years was a way of protecting myself. Anger gave me the strength to fight off my dad's last attempt to hurt me. Anger had seeped into my pores and caused me to hate myself. Even suicide had felt like a good option. In my head, I knew the anger was causing me to break down, but I didn't know how to be free of it.

"Do you want to accept Jesus into your life, Jessica? Wait … are you okay?" Janice questioned me as a darkness filled my eyes and emotion left my face.

"Are you ready to accept Jesus?" she repeated.

"No!" The anger took over. I suddenly wanted to take everything out on Janice and Noelle. I felt like I was losing control. I ran to the kitchen and snatched a butcher knife.

"Pray, pray, pray," Janice instructed Noelle. The two began to ask God to release me from my rage and the seemingly demonic force inside me.

I came running back to the bedroom where we had been talking, heading straight for them, but just as I was about to lunge at them with the knife, I turned the knife around and pointed it behind me. *What am I doing?!* I thought to myself. *Jesus, help me!*

"Yes! I want Jesus!" I shouted as I fell to my knees in front of Janice. "Yes!"

It all happened so quickly. *I threatened them with a knife,* I thought. *That was crazy.* I immediately began to pray with Janice, asking God to come into my life and forgive me for my anger and for all the things I'd done wrong. As I prayed, my pulse settled, and I felt peace from the darkness I'd been carrying. The weight of the rage lifted and left me feeling exhausted. I was sweating.

For years, I convinced myself that God wouldn't want me because of things my dad made me do. I convinced myself that God didn't love me and would never love me, but I was wrong. I knew I was wrong because in that moment with God, all I felt was overwhelming and abundant love from him. As much as I had tried to refuse him, even taking off my shoes to avoid going to the altar with bare feet, I received the love he had for me, and I tried with all of my might to love myself as well.

❧❧❧

Living in Tampa presented a new struggle for me. I was going to church regularly while continuing to learn about Jesus and study the Bible, but I had a hard time adjusting at school. There were more than 3,000 students in my 11ᵗʰ grade class. I'd come from a school with 500 students total. Noelle and I begged our moms to let us move back to Louisiana and promised we would keep going to church and school. Both of them agreed to let us go in February of our junior year, so we moved home and stayed at the house Noelle's family still owned there and with other friends.

Janice or Bill came home at least one weekend a month, so they were checking in on us, but it was apparent we weren't keeping our end of the deal. I was what I called a "yo-yo Christian," meaning I went back and forth between building a relationship with God and then avoiding him and doing whatever I felt like. When we left Tampa and went home, we planned to go back and tell all our friends about Jesus, but we ended up hanging out with friends at a bar on Friday and Saturday nights. Sometimes we'd take those same friends to church with us on Sundays.

Janice knew I'd had a problem with drinking and smoking, so she started praying that I would no longer desire or physically tolerate those things. Soon, the smell and taste of cigarettes gave me a headache. Later, drinking made me sick, no matter how little I drank. I was annoyed but not deterred. I tried continuing to smoke and drink, but I definitely didn't enjoy doing either as much and began to cut back.

Noelle's parents realized we weren't doing well on our own. We stayed some with friends and a few of Noelle's family members, so we weren't always completely unsupervised, but her parents knew we'd do better if they returned home. They moved back to Louisiana during our senior year.

I was busy working and paying all of my private school tuition and my car insurance and gas. Noelle's parents provided me with food and shelter, but my mom was busy trying to support herself and my younger brothers.

I was disappointed when my mom eventually returned to Louisiana and went back to my dad.

"He's changed," she tried convincing me, knowing he had hit rock bottom when she left him and he lost everything. "He really has changed."

I wasn't so convinced.

❧❧❧

My "yo-yo Christianity" continued. Not long before graduating from high school, I was looking forward to our senior trip to Mexico. I also wanted to attend summer Bible school in Dallas before starting classes at Louisiana State University that fall. Both deposits were due at the same time, and I didn't have enough money for both.

I knew the trip to Florida would be filled with partying, and I had plans to hook up with a guy I knew. The trip would probably involve a lot of drinking and drugs — things I knew weren't good for me.

I also knew that Bible school would be something that God would want me to do, and I would be given the chance to learn and grow.

It seemed like God was giving me a choice. *Follow after what feels good and choose death. Or follow me and choose life.*

I was pretty sure I wasn't going to actually die if I went to Florida, but I was certain that the trip would be a straight path to spiritual death. I'd refused God so many times in my life, but I knew that this decision would help determine my future.

I didn't want to be a "yo-yo Christian" anymore. Jesus had saved me over and over again — from my own rage, from my poor choices, from myself. I loved him like a friend, and I knew he only wanted what was best for me.

I made my decision. I wanted to follow after Jesus.

৵৵৵

"There is a young girl here tonight who hates her father," the man declared. "You were sexually abused by your father, and you hate him. And because you hate him and can't forgive him, you can't receive God's forgiveness."

I had gone to the optional Bible school event that evening to hear a guest speaker but didn't expect to be singled out from the crowd.

"Because you can't receive God's forgiveness, you keep going back and forth between the world and God," he continued.

No way. He knows I'm a "yo-yo Christian."

"You need to forgive your dad, so you can be forgiven and live fully for God."

I couldn't believe he knew my heart with such detail. I began crying while still in my seat, blown away by how powerful God's message was for me, coming from a man I'd never met and who knew nothing about me.

"Come forward," he said blindly, not knowing who he was speaking to in the crowd.

I went forward and was greeted by a small group of people at the altar. Each person prayed for me as I fell to my knees, and my quiet tears turned to sobs. I let myself forgive my dad for what he had done. That night, I fully embraced the truth: I could forgive my dad for what he had done to me even if he hadn't asked me for forgiveness. My forgiveness was not determined by his wanting to be forgiven but by my willingness to get my own heart right with God and move forward with the life he had in store for me.

The people at the altar continued to pray for me. I'd

kept my tears locked up tight since the night I'd placed my teddy bear on my nightstand. I'd decided that I would never cry again about what I had endured at the hands of my dad. But in that moment, I sobbed and released it all. I cried at the altar for two hours as my heart softened, and I truly forgave him. At the end of the night, I no longer felt like I had to hold him accountable for what he did to me.

I went home and wrote my dad a letter and let him know that what he did was wrong, but I was no longer going to hold it against him. I told him I forgave him, and he needed to seek forgiveness for himself. Whether or not he sought forgiveness from God or from me was his choice, just as it had been my choice to forgive him.

My dad never responded directly to the letter, but months later at my younger brother's graduation, he acknowledged receiving it in his own way.

"Thanks," he said, hugging me and smiling.

৵৵৵

I chose not to go to Louisiana State University and opted to remain at Bible college instead. Life was changing quickly, and I soon met a man who was handsome and funny and came from a strong Christian family.

"This is for you," Jonas said, handing me a rose. He stood on my front porch at Bible college, my roommates swooning at his romantic gesture, inviting me to go for a walk with him.

"I'd love to," I answered, also swooning.

As we talked along our walk, I felt the enormity of why he wanted to share what was in his heart.

"God told me when I was 16 that I was not supposed to date until I met the right person — the person I am going to marry," he explained. He had never strayed from his commitment to God. "God told me I needed to save myself and wait on him to bring me the right person. You're the person I want to date."

"Wait a minute," I said, chuckling. "Are you proposing?"

"Not exactly. I just need you to know what this means to me."

I'd never met a man like Jonas before. I still struggled with trusting men, even though I had forgiven my dad. Jonas obviously loved God and trusted him with his life. His faith helped to ease my distrust. It didn't take long for me to fall in love.

Ours was a sweet courtship. We both remained obedient to what Jonas believed God had asked of him, and we waited to be intimate until we were married 18 months later. I asked my dad to give me away, and he did. Both my parents were at our wedding.

Surrounded by our family and friends, I realized that when I'd chosen God, I'd made room for God to heal the oldest, deepest wound of my heart. He helped me to forgive my dad and gave me a loving husband I knew I could trust.

ৡৡৡ

After we married, Jonas and I moved to Oregon, where Jonas and his family were from. We eventually ended up in Prineville, Oregon, and began attending Eastside Church.

Our time at Eastside Church became a growing experience for me. Eastside Church tries to help each person thrive and become who God wants them to be by following God's agenda, not their own agenda. As I let church elders know I could be available to support other women who have suffered sexual abuse, they supported my efforts and helped make a difference in the lives of women who may not otherwise feel understood or able to forgive.

As Jonas and I continued our walk with the Lord, I considered God's agenda for me. I considered what would have become of my life if I had chosen to go on the graduation trip instead of listening to God and choosing to use the money to attend Bible school the summer before I met Jonas. If I hadn't gone to Bible school, I wouldn't have attended the event that led me to forgive my dad. I wouldn't have met my husband during a time of enormous healing in my life. And I am certain I wouldn't have had the strength, faith or ability to be the parent I am today.

Jonas grew up in a Christian home, never wavering from his commitment to God, and I have learned from his example. Today, as a mother and wife, I have been blessed to share my life with a man who nurtures and loves his family, resolves conflict in a healthy way and shows patience in times of strife. My children trust in their father, while learning of God's love for them and his place in their lives.

I believe God nudged me to go to Bible school the summer before attending Bible college because he was preparing my life for meeting Jonas. After all the years I spent thinking God wouldn't want me, I'd finally realized that God not only wanted me, but he also wanted me to share my life with an honorable and godly man.

It's called a fork in the road for a reason. Because we can point back to a pivotal time in our lives and know that nearly everything before and after that crossing defined who we would become. I am so grateful I chose the wonderful path.

OUT OF THE KETTLE
The Story of James
Written by Douglas Abbott

Everything changed in a split second. One moment, I was laughing with my friends in the "man cave," feeling the chemically induced euphoria rush into my head. The next, I turned around to see Becky standing right behind me. Her hazel eyes were wide with shock and hurt.

"I … Hi, honey. What are you doing in here?"

Becky said nothing, but her eyes spoke volumes.

The cat was out of the bag. The secret I'd kept successfully from my wife was out in the open like a rotting corpse. The evidence was plain as day on the table before me — the mirror in the center of it still bore several thick lines of sparkling white powder.

I tried to speak, but no words came. What could I say? *Honey, I meant to tell you that I'm a coke freak, but I was just waiting for the right time.* My face was hot with shame.

Becky turned and quietly walked out of the room.

❧❧❧

I never thought about the peculiarity of my having three sets of grandparents. I just thought it was cool. Somehow, I glossed over it each time Grandma Rollins referred to "Daddy Dale" when I was visiting with her. I had some vague awareness that the man she referred to lived down in California. However, I didn't learn that he was my biological father until I was 8. The realization had no effect on me.

The man I called "Dad" was a wonderful father, though Mother disapproved of his periodic drinking binges, not merely for moral reasons but also because of the expense. Once, I heard my dad return home around midnight. Something about his footfalls told me he had been drinking. I heard Mom stomp into the kitchen to confront him. Her voice was shrill with profanities, and I heard the sound of pottery breaking, followed by the slamming of the door. I learned the next day that Mom broke a bowl over Dad's head and shoved him outside the house.

These kinds of incidents were rare — and never during my early elementary school years — and were of no great concern to me. I grew up believing all was well with the world.

I had three sisters — one older, two younger. We couldn't have defined the word "poor," though that's what we were, according to the usual definition. We didn't think about the fact that Dad had to work four jobs to ensure that we never went hungry.

Mom and Dad both imparted a strong work ethic to us. "Regardless of what you have (or don't have), you get after it and make the most of it" was often heard in our house. The words penetrated because my parents were the first to heed them.

OUT OF THE KETTLE

❧❧❧

Everything changed in the summer of 1978. It was well after dark when something jarred me awake. I lay in bed clutching my covers and felt an electric tension hanging in the air. I heard the dogs barking, then the thuds of Dad's feet hitting the porch. A few moments later, I heard my mother's voice, high with fright. Then three successive explosions caused me to sit straight up in my bed. Suddenly, the house filled with the sounds of distress as Mom and my sisters howled and ran for the door. I was close behind them.

As soon as I was on the porch, I looked out into the yard and saw a young man sprawled on the ground, holding his leg. Dad stood 10 or 15 feet away pointing a rifle at him.

We lived in a small town in Eastern Oregon, where news travels a bit slower than electricity. Within minutes, the sheriff and several deputies were on the scene, and neighbors clustered about.

"… can't go around shooting people, Fred." The sheriff's hands were on his hips.

"I told you, I wasn't trying to hit him!" Dad almost yelled. "I was aiming at the ground."

"Well, why did you fire to begin with?"

"He was trying to climb through my daughter's window. Then he ignored me when I told him to stop. If you ask me, he got off easy."

The intruder was a 19-year-old local named Jeffrey

with designs on my older sister. Before the situation could be sorted out, his father arrived on the scene and started screaming death threats against my father.

"I've got to take you into custody, Fred." The sheriff's face was tight.

"Take *me* in? What for?"

"For your own safety."

Patty stood off to the side, screaming, "I hate you!" at Dad over and over. Mom kept telling her to stop, but she just screamed all the louder.

I watched with bewilderment as Sheriff Jones drove away with my father in the passenger seat. Just before they pulled away, I motioned to Dad to roll the window down, and he did.

"I love you, Dad." There were tears in my eyes.

"I love you, too, son."

From that day on, my family was in splinters. Two days after the shooting, my younger sisters and I were in the car with Mom as we drove past Grandma Rollins' house. As we passed by the driveway, we saw Jeffrey headed into the house, still walking on crutches. We had no idea why he was there, but it seemed like a betrayal to even permit him on the premises.

"Look at that," Mom muttered, shaking her head. "She's more worried about that predator than she is you kids. I can't believe she hasn't even called to ask how you guys are doing."

The second Mom uttered the words, unforgiveness lodged in my heart.

Up to that time, Grandma Rollins had been one of my favorite people. She often looked after us while Mom and Dad worked.

I spent countless hours in her kitchen enjoying lemonade and cookies while she told me stories about her upbringing or building forts in her yard. Now, I was confused about whether a relationship with her would betray my mom and dad. I abruptly stopped calling and visiting and gave no explanation. It was as though she no longer existed. In the following weeks and months, I learned that Grandma Rollins was hurt and bewildered over my rejection. But I didn't even think about changing my posture toward her.

Patty, true to her word, had nothing but hatred for Dad. Almost immediately after the shooting, she went down to Children's Services Division and filed a report of abuse against him.

My sisters and I had all been spanked by my parents at one time or another, but the way I saw it, none of it could reasonably be called abuse. I never felt singled out or brutalized. To the contrary, I always had it coming.

There was an immediate, full-tilt investigation, and a caseworker arrived to take Patty away to foster care. I thought about striking him with a baseball bat as he followed her out the door with one of her suitcases. Then I watched with dismay and anger as they stowed the luggage and drove away. She would be gone for three years.

Other grownups showed up and took us to the CSD office for separate interviews. I ended up sitting and talking with a strange sallow-faced man. He sat across from me scribbling on his legal pad.

"So James — may I call you Jim? — Jim, how often do you receive spankings from your parents? Mmmm-hmmmm. And how severe are they?"

There were many other questions, all of them intrusive. I wondered what was happening to my family. I replayed the shooting in my mind many times. Each time I did, I was afraid of what Jeffrey's father might do. Would he make good on his threats? He was enraged because his son had been shot. Was it possible he might take his anger out on me? I was the counterpart to his son. It seemed to me that coming after me made the most logical sense.

I lived with that fear, especially at night, when the darkness could conceal anything. I was petrified whenever I had to go out after nightfall. One of my chores was taking out the trash. Instead of taking it clear to the curb, I would stay as close to the porch as possible and pitch the bag at the barrel. If it landed on the ground, that was where it stayed.

Although there was tension in our house, my parents actually posted the number for CSD by the phone and said we could call it if we wanted. They would not fight it again. Everyone was aware of the hole that had been created by Patty's departure. The family held together, but we all knew that, regardless of the outcome of the investigation, everything had changed permanently.

Life is strange. Rejection that is more perceived than real can ruin a person just as handily. During this time, I quickly adjusted to a new code I couldn't have even put into words. As I understood in some visceral way, the Hallmark world of giving, embracing and trusting was a lie — a contrivance. The real world consisted of people who hurt and others who foolishly consented to being hurt. I could sidestep all of it. All I had to do was remember one rule: You trust yourself, and forget everyone else. All these distorted convictions — which I never once evaluated or questioned — became my way of life. I learned quickly to devalue everyone but myself.

৵৵৵

I got drunk for the first time at age 16. Even years later, the experience seemed like a fluke. I grew up around alcohol and had never had any great desire to drink to excess. Nor was I seeking relief from emotional pain. It just happened that some high school friends I was spending the evening with had a large quantity of beer. Once I started tossing them back, I simply kept going until I couldn't walk. It felt great, but I later became deathly ill and had a dream in which a swarm of hornets engulfed me. Each time one of them stung me, I heard a sound like a car horn.

Getting sick from drinking didn't make me think twice about doing it again — I just drank less.

During that same year, I lost my virginity almost offhandedly. Lana was a year older and attractive. Being pursued by her was an invigorating experience. However, it didn't take me very long to transition to the next girl. It was the early '80s, and the teenagers I knew thought you were dull and unpopular if you weren't having sex. Like many of my peers, I had a list of girls I worked from. I wasn't about to be left behind.

Hence, I was fully launched into the world of social drinking and promiscuity. Neither activity was particularly enjoyable; it was all about reaching for manhood. I stopped short of experimenting with drugs. Between the statements of my parents and the education campaign at school, I believed drugs were dangerous and steered clear of them, even though many of my peers were plunging into that world with abandon.

I failed to connect the dots between my behavior and the adversarial relationship I suddenly developed with the law. Over the next couple of years, I was cited four times — once for using a fake ID in a bar and three times for possessing beer as a minor. I had the same attitude as so many other young men who were doing the same things — that the police should be out catching criminals instead of harassing me.

Dad noticed what was happening and sat me down for a talk.

"Son, we need to talk about sex."

I paused, then asked, "What do you want to know?"

"Okay," Dad said. Just okay. And that was that. Almost.

"No, there's one other thing. Have you ever thought about the military?"

I humored Dad for five seconds because I respected him. However, I saw no need for change. I was about to graduate from high school and was already making good money as a firefighter for the Forest Service. I rarely partied except on the weekends.

I took no heed when my parents evicted me for throwing a party in the house. I had just returned to town for the weekend to find my parents and younger sisters gone on vacation. That night, the house was packed with teenagers and young adults, all clutching plastic cups of beer and gyrating to earsplitting rock music.

It was a counter-culture free-for-all, with couples making enthusiastic use of every private space in the house — including my parents' bed.

Before I was able to get the mess cleaned up, I received a call from dispatch with the Forest Service and was off for another gig. Six days later, I called Mom to ask for a ride back home from the compound.

"I'll be there," she said abruptly and hung up.

It was very quiet in the car as we started back. But tension was building.

"Look," Mom said finally, "all your things are packed up at the house. Don't even bother asking why. You blew it. Dad and I are willing to let you stay on a probationary basis, but you're going to have to start respecting our rules."

My heart was hard. "Well, it looks to me like you already made up your mind. You packed my stuff, so I'll go." The decision was of little consequence; I was leaving for school in a few months, anyway. I could stay with friends until then.

꙰꙰꙰

I moved to the Willamette Valley to attend a small college in the fall of 1984. I honestly intended to earn a degree and even joined the baseball team. However, I immediately fell in with a hard-partying crowd and expanded my favorite pastime to include weekdays. Without any thought about my former position on the dangers of drugs, I began experimenting with crystal meth, cocaine and magic mushrooms. Before long, school was an inconvenience. Whenever there was a conflict between my drinking schedule and my class requirements, I resented the latter.

One of my friends in the dormitory was a math major. Randy heard me complaining one evening about having to go to class the next morning — hung over, as usual.

"Hey, I can cover for you," he offered. By this, he meant attend the class for me.

"No! It would never work. If the instructor is there, he'll spot you from a mile away."

"Well, if he is, I'll just leave. But if he has a TA there, I can take the exam for you."

I agreed to the arrangement and slept my hangover off while Randy aced my exam. However, at the end of the next class, my professor stopped me before I could get out of the room.

"Mr. Reynolds, I'm a little concerned." He handed me the test Randy had taken for me. He had scored 100 percent.

"Instructors get a little nervous when there is a dramatic shift in a student's work. Would you mind just sitting down and doing a few problems for me?" He handed me a different sheet.

My face grew hot. The problems looked like writing in a foreign language.

"You know I can't do those," I said after a pause.

Professor Jenkins nodded. "I know. You pick your friends well." He put his hands in his pockets. "By all rights, you should be expelled from the university for cheating. But I'm going to give you an opportunity to make this right."

However, even with makeup exams, I ended up with a failing grade in the class. I would need to retake the class the following term to keep my GPA from tanking. Not that I was taking my studies seriously; my only aim was to stay off academic probation so I could continue playing baseball.

My promiscuity continued, and I had another clash with the law — again for drinking.

During that first reckless semester of college, the inevitable occurred.

"I'm pregnant," Suzanne told me over the phone.

What do you expect me to do about it? I thought. Suzanne and I weren't even seeing each other regularly. All we had done was meet from time to time for sex.

"How do you know it's mine?"

"I haven't been with anyone else."

"Well, I'm not convinced it's mine," I said, to end the conversation. Truthfully, there was no evidence to the contrary. However, admitting I had impregnated her would obligate me to help her deal with the pregnancy. I had a habit of getting rid of unsavory realities by denying them.

I learned later that she terminated the pregnancy.

There is an old saying that if a frog is placed in boiling water, it will jump out. But if it is placed in cold water that is slowly heated, it will not perceive the danger and will be cooked to death.

In all these things — my ramped-up drinking, drugs, loveless sex, blowing off my class requirements and all the attendant repercussions — I turned a blind eye.

స్త్రోస్త్రోస్త్రో

I dropped out of school in the spring of 1985 and returned to my hometown to find work. With a single phone call, I got back on with the Forest Service and was soon working in the woods every day.

Provided I did my job, I could drink all I wanted in my off hours and could even smoke pot on the clock. The Forest Service didn't drug test, and we usually worked alone in the woods.

Then, missing my college friends, I moved back to the Valley again. While I was couch surfing, I hooked back up with my first girlfriend, Carly. After I had been seeing her sporadically for a few months, she called to tell me she was pregnant.

Knowing she was sexually active, I took the same approach I had used with the girl from college.

"Why do you think it's mine?"

"I *know* it's yours."

"How?"

"Because I know."

"You call that proof?"

I heard her voice break. "I can't believe you slept with me, and now you're talking to me about proof! It doesn't matter what you say. I know it's yours." And she hung up.

The next time I saw her, I saw sadness in her eyes. She wouldn't even look at me. I learned later that she had gotten an abortion.

After staying with various friends over a period of several months, I got a job at a mill in a nearby town. The hours were often long, and most of the workers used crystal meth to get through the shifts. Then, after the whistle blew in the evening, most of us headed for a local bar to indulge our appetites for cold beer and fast girls.

I met my first wife, Candace, in a nightclub. I spotted her from clear across the bar playing pool and wiggling to a Robert Palmer tune. She was the spitting image of Courtney Cox, with clear blue eyes and short brunette hair. I followed her into the ladies' room to strike up a conversation with her.

Candace and I hit it off famously. Over the next few

weeks, I spent so much time over at her apartment that she suggested I move in.

"You're here all the time. You might as well share the rent," one of her roommates agreed.

Candace was going to school to be an elementary school teacher. While she finished up her studies, I continued working in the mill. We tied the knot in the summer of 1987 and moved to Central Oregon, where Candace had been hired as a teacher. I quickly got hired at a mill in the area and picked up where I'd left off in the Valley — using meth during the day and hitting the bars in the evening.

To this day, I don't fully understand why we got married. Neither of us had the first clue about relationships. We had little in common other than our enthusiasm for the nightlife. We scarcely knew each other. Within a year, we were both having extramarital affairs and were soon separated.

Although I was just as guilty as Candace, I blamed the split on her and even felt rejected.

I moved into an apartment with three of my friends from the mill. We all used cocaine and crystal meth and drank like fish. Our house quickly gained a reputation as a party house. Whenever we were there, other people were there, also, always in some stage of intoxication.

Before long, I noticed I was always broke because of my drug use. So I started selling cocaine to our party guests to make ends meet. Regardless, I was always running out of money.

OUT OF THE KETTLE

I never once thought about reforming my habits. Whatever I was feeling, it was easy enough to whisk away with a six-pack of beer and a few lines of coke. Besides, what was happening in my gut had nothing to do with reality. Rent, food and an ample supply of beer and cocaine — that was reality.

I was looking more and more like the frog in the kettle — immersed in water that was just coming to a boil. By this time, I considered it normal to be high or intoxicated most of the time. Likewise, I hardly noticed the regular legal trouble and the personal strife that was an almost daily occurrence. In a particularly brazen display, I earned 30 days in jail for drunkenly assaulting a complete stranger in a bar in the town of John Day. I might have forgotten about the incident entirely, except that the authorities tracked me to Madras and arrested me at work. My attorney informed me that, in addition to the month in the slammer, I would be on the hook for significant restitution. I had managed to knock several of the guy's teeth out.

 ༄ ༄ ༄

I met Becky in the summer of 1989. She was working at a pharmacy and was training to be a nanny. She was beautiful — petite and slender, with gorgeous brunette locks. I was physically attracted, but I was also drawn to something wholesome in her that represented the exact opposite of what I was — a scoundrel. I couldn't have put it into words, but I saw something in her that I wanted —

something peaceful and gentle I had never gotten a glimpse of before. So I kept after her until she consented to a date with me. Why she agreed, I'll never know. She was a good girl, and I was a hard-drinking, drug-using bum. I suppose I wore her down with my charm. Five months later, we finally went on our first date.

This was an entirely new kind of relationship for me. I had more regard for this one woman than for all the others I had ever been with *combined*. Early on, she disclosed how she had been with some callous, utterly self-centered guys. She had been hurt. For the first time, I wanted to protect a woman instead of ravaging her. I resolved that I was going to be the gentlest, most considerate person I could be with her. I was not going to hurt her at all or give her any reason to question whether she could trust me.

In a way I could not yet understand, I was seeking to rejoin the human race. It just happened that Becky was the catalyst. Before I met her, I was content to stomp through others' lives as though they didn't matter. Becky was the first person to matter to me in a very long time.

In the meantime, however, I was still immature and self-centered. In my distorted thinking at the time, I could be this reformed, gallant man without giving up my substances. I would just make sure to keep them away from Becky.

That was how our relationship began. After a bit of clumsiness and squaring off, something clicked, and we began spending all our free time together.

OUT OF THE KETTLE

Two years later, we got married. With money we had earmarked specifically for our honeymoon, we went off on a Caribbean cruise and had the time of our lives.

Our son Jeremy was born in 1992.

Becky was unaware that I was still using drugs secretly, though not as much as I had before. Whatever doubts or fears she may have had were swept under the daily barrage of life's increasing demands.

However, a reckoning came in 1993.

Becky and I were social creatures and went out in the evening when we could find a sitter for Jeremy. I had an old friend with a big house who often invited us to come to his parties. There were always several couples in attendance, mostly married. Normally, after snacks and a few drinks in the living room, the men would leave the women and move to the garage, where we would lock the door, crank the music, play pool and continue drinking beer. It was then that the mirror came out.

We went to Phil's one particular Friday after a grueling week. Around 8 p.m., the men retired to the garage as usual, and the mirror came out right away.

A chorus of enthusiasm went up, and everyone reached for his wallet to chip in. A pile of bills was placed on the table as the mirror was loaded.

I had never lost my taste for cocaine, not even after all the money I had spent on it over the years. It never failed to deliver a sharp explosion of energy and excitement. It was perfect for balancing out the beer.

It was 9:30, and I had just taken a drink of beer when I

looked up to see bleached, embarrassed expressions on my friends' faces. They were all staring behind me. I turned around to see Becky standing in the door. We had forgotten to lock it. Right in the middle of the table in front of us sat the mirror, covered with lines.

I stammered something nonsensical, but there was nothing to say. Everyone in the room knew what was happening. Slowly, without comment, Becky turned and walked back into the living room.

The next morning, I sat at the breakfast table and nibbled listlessly at a slice of toast. Becky sat across from me reading the newspaper and sipping coffee. The tension was unbearable.

Finally, she looked up and fixed her hazel eyes on me. "It's got to stop, Jim. I'm not going to raise my child around drugs. You have a choice to make: the drugs or me and Jeremy."

Rejection was my great fear. I had spent most of my life as an emotional recluse to avoid it. At long last, my heart had opened to permit this woman and now my infant son into my life. I couldn't imagine living without them. I would do whatever I had to do.

Becky and I continued to drink recreationally, but I never touched another drug after that. Strangely, once I made the break, I didn't miss it terribly.

Our second son, Nolan, was born in 1995. It was a joyous but solemn moment. In four years of marriage, I had of necessity shed a great deal of selfishness and irresponsibility. For the first time, I watched Becky being stretched to the limit. I knew she needed more help from me. It was a moment of truth.

At about the same time, my mother-in-law brought over some of Becky's things from her basement. There were several boxes, and one of them contained stacks of scrapbook materials. Becky had never gotten around to actually putting them into a book. One quiet evening at home, we ate spaghetti and garlic bread and began pulling mementos out of the box. There were old diaries, notes from old boyfriends, dog-eared photographs and another item that would change our lives: In the very bottom of the box was a decorative pencil box. Becky gave a little gasp when she saw it.

The box contained a stack of letters wrapped in a ribbon. Letters to God. Becky had written them when she was a teen.

"I was in love with Jesus then." Becky looked as though she might weep. "I don't know what happened."

She lifted the crinkled pages from the box, untied the ribbon and sat down to read them. From the first one, several dried petals fell out as she unfolded it — a white rose pressed into the paper by her young hand.

Dear God,

It's funny, but I can't remember when I wasn't aware of you. How empty my life must have been before you came into it! You have taught me so much in the last year, how wonderful life can be. I see you everywhere now.

I need you to help me forgive. I don't understand hurtful people, why they do the things they do. Shawn handled my heart like it was garbage. I still want to claw his eyes out. But I know you want me to forgive him. Help me to pray for him every night. I know you love him.

Love,
Becky

As she read the letter, something shifted inside me. I thought about the many girls I had used for my own pleasure. Their pain was an untold story. Some of them had surely cried themselves to sleep because of my callousness. I hadn't even seen their humanity before.

But there was another layer to this. Here was a young girl, heartbroken but refusing to stop trusting in God. I imagined Jesus standing beside her, smiling with pleasure as she wrote letters to him.

I had grown up believing in the existence of God and Jesus. However, I had never known them. But as Becky read her letters to me that evening, with spaghetti sauce drying on the plates in the kitchen, I saw it for the first time: God was *real*. He loved every one of us with an eternal love and was waiting like a gentleman off to the side — waiting for us to reach out to him. His love was more real than the cruelest person, the greatest tragedy.

Things began to change. Becky began searching for a church, and after she had been attending for a few weeks, I was amazed at the change in her.

Then she started bringing home videos from the Brownsville Revival. This was 1996, when something called the Pensacola Outpouring was fresh and dramatic. We sat in our living room and watched people getting baptized and shaking from what they regarded as the direct touch of God. I had grown up attending a strict church, but I wasn't unnerved by the outlandish things we saw on the videos. I didn't question for a second that it was real. I wanted what was happening to them.

Finally, Becky came home from a women's retreat exhausted but glowing. Something very significant had happened to her. However, it was a week later before she finally told me what it was.

"I gave my life back to Jesus, James." Her eyes danced with joy. "Everything's going to be all right. It's going to be better than all right. I'm SAVED!"

As her teenage letters to God had disclosed, Becky had walked with God and fallen away into promiscuity. She never spoke about what had caused her to falter, but it was the source of great sorrow in her life. She ardently desired to walk with Jesus again but had felt paralyzed — ashamed of her desertion. However, during this retreat, she had heard God's voice in an unmistakable way. *I still love you, child. You're going to be fine. I have you right in my hand. Nothing can harm you or keep you away from me.*

I couldn't understand why it had taken a week for Becky to tell me about her experience at the retreat. Was I such a cold fish that she expected a negative response?

Something had to change. From that time on, I knew I

was going after this Jesus who loved so tirelessly. He was what I had needed my entire life.

In that spring of 1996, I committed my life to Christ, and everything was immediately on a different footing.

Becky and I discovered Eastside Church and were soon more plugged in with the congregation than I had known it was possible for one family to be. It seemed like we were there every time the doors were open.

In addition to services and activities, Becky started serving in preschool ministries, and I became an usher. Most significantly, I enrolled in a series of classes called Cleansing Streams at the church. The entire course centered on God's forgiveness. As I studied the scriptures, a wholly new side of God came into view — a being who had given his son over to a barbaric death in order to make a way for *me*. Not only that, but even after such a monumental sacrifice, this God continued to patiently minister to people who often ignored and disobeyed him. I got a glimpse of love and loyalty I had previously dismissed as the stuff of romance novels.

Through these studies, I saw my unforgiveness and how it had controlled me.

I had been consumed by fear and rejection because of my biological father's abandonment, then in turn the dismantling of my family after the shooting. These negative forces had colored my life from an early age, but I hadn't even known they were there. However, as I acknowledged them and asked God to remove them, their oppressive power began to be lifted from me.

Our church became our extended family. I served on the church council, taught Sunday school and got involved with the church's youth ministry. From the time we arrived there, we have been integrally involved in the activities and ministries. I say this not boastfully, but with gratitude. Our service has benefited us more than it has Eastside Church.

Our family grew again when our daughter Miriam was born in 1998. We were aware then that it was more important than ever for us to keep our family together. Becky and I spoke openly about generational curses and the rampant divorce in my family. We prayed for strength to stay together, no matter what came.

This commitment was to be tested sorely in later years when Becky and I decided to open a coffee shop. For the first six months, everything went well. Business was booming. Then, three other coffee shops opened nearby. Business suffered. Becky's workload doubled as she both worked the floor and managed the business for seven years. During that time, I served at the church and worked as a production manager at a mill in Madras, but I had nothing like the burden that Becky suffered. We have discussed writing a book about those years — *Hell Looks Like a Coffee Shop*. Her suffering, and the attendant stress it placed on our marriage, drove us deeper into prayer. Through that time, and over the last 20 years, God has been faithful. We have never lacked for anything we needed, material or spiritual.

The wholesomeness of our children's lives stands in

contrast to the destructive choices Becky and I made when we were young.

I haven't been bashful about discussing the waywardness of my youth. I mention those early choices frequently when I minister to young people. I shared my story at church recently.

"Young people, God knows all about your curiosity, your sexual desires, the pressure that is placed on you out there to experiment with drugs. He isn't trying to stifle you. He wants to satisfy your desires with good things! His commands are there to protect you. I'm here to tell you that there is nothing satisfying to be found in promiscuity and drug abuse. You don't have to go through the things I did. I have mentioned them often enough. All I got out of it was pain and guilt because of how my actions affected others. God wants to spare you all that.

"You may be suffering under some other burden — depression, loneliness or anger. God's arm isn't too short to deal with any of it. I lived in a cage of my own making for many, many years. I was rejected by my biological father and lived in fear. Whatever it is, God can take you out from under it. You just have to trust him.

"You say, how could it be so simple? I'm telling you that God's favor is a gift to all of us. Jesus desires a relationship with us. It's that simple. Some of you have already dabbled in drugs and sex. You don't have to clean up or get right before you start your relationship with Christ. He wants you to come to him right now, as you are.

"Let us remember the words of our Savior: 'Come to me, all you who are weary and heavy-laden, and I will give you rest. Take my yoke upon you and learn from me. For I am gentle and humble in heart, and you will find rest for your souls. For my yoke is easy and my burden is light'" (Matthew 11:28-30).

To this day, it blows me away how God reached out to me again and again — even as I completely ignored him. I am living proof that God loves the unlovable.

TRAGEDY AT INDIAN LAKE
The Story of Lee
Written by Chrissy Spallone

Let me tell you about prejudice. I faced many challenges as a blond, blue-eyed girl married to an American Indian, but my husband, Henry, and I learned to get past it. At least my parents accepted our relationship — they'd already gotten to know Henry through his friendship with the boy next door. He stopped by our house often to chat with my dad and later admitted he was always trying to get a look at me. Sadly, others weren't so accepting.

Henry attracted me from the start. He stood tall and beautiful, with high cheekbones and dark olive skin. I thought he looked a lot like Elvis. But despite his good looks, people would harass us when we went places together, and most landlords didn't want to rent to us. Sometimes the kids and I went house hunting by ourselves, but once the landlord found out he'd rented to a Native American, the harassment would start. We tried to make the best of it, like the time the landlord flooded out our entire yard to irrigate it instead of simply using a sprinkler like normal. Henry just smiled and said, "All right, kids, get your swimming gear, and let's enjoy this nice water they've provided for us!"

Our marriage endured more struggles than most, but

we stood strong in the face of them all. And yet, nothing could have prepared us for the shock that came in the spring of 1978, when Henry and I found ourselves under investigation for murder. We were sitting in a hospital room with policemen all around us, asking all sorts of questions. One of them asked, "Did you kill your children on purpose?"

It took my husband and two officers to pry me off of him. After all we'd been through, it was the wrong thing to say.

❧❧❧

I married young. Before meeting Henry, I didn't stray far from my parents' home in Portland, Oregon. I was born in 1951 and lived a rather typical '50s childhood. My parents and older brother loved me, and I never went without anything I really needed. My grandparents lived close by, and Grandma made all my clothes by hand until my junior year of high school.

I spent a lot of time with my grandparents, but especially my grandfather, whom I considered my hero. I was told he used to drive an old Model T. And after that broke down, he walked everywhere. I can still remember watching him walk up the road coming home from work. Then, he'd give me a hug and let me know I was his special little girl.

Childhood fun was simple back then. A nearby dairy farm shut down early in my youth, but the big barn remained, as did a giant cement water trough for the cows, and we kids went in and cleaned it out and made it our swimming pool.

Everyone near us owned lots of land, and the tree-lined streets gave the impression of a magical tunnel when we drove or walked around the neighborhood.

My mother used to drop me off at church every week so I could go to Sunday school with the other kids, and I went there for a while. I stopped going when I reached the age of 12.

That was the same time my grandfather died.

My grandfather developed a brain tumor and went to stay at a nursing home. I think I only got to visit him once, and at that point he wasn't the same grandfather I knew. Doctors did something drastic to reduce his great pain, and that robbed him of his ability to speak. He just wasn't there anymore. I prayed and prayed because they taught me at church that God answers prayer, but it didn't go as I expected. He passed away in 1963.

Following my grandfather's death, I slipped into a stage of adolescent rebellion. I considered it a big deal at the time, having always been a good girl, but it mirrored what many other teens go through. I started cussing a lot, and by the time I turned 16, I started drinking alcohol and smoking cigarettes that my friends would give me. My grades didn't suffer from any of this. I still earned A's and B's, and I volunteered in a local hospital through a candy striper course my high school offered. I don't know if schools offer that anymore, but we all wore a cute little blue-and-white-striped nurse's dress, back in the days when nurses still wore dresses, and a hat to match. I was the only candy striper around, and staff members took me under their wings and let me do all sorts of things, like taking X-rays. I did so much more than empty bedpans and fold sheets.

When I took a paying job as a nurse's aide, I did almost everything. When people died, I would take care of them and wash them and clean them. It messed with my head a little bit. I witnessed several patients die. It looked to me like their deaths were due to neglect by the staff, and that just didn't seem right. I took an interest in herbology and natural medicine. I learned a lot of illnesses could be healed with garlic and honey and other herbs. But natural remedies can't cure everything.

That's how I spent my childhood in Portland. When we lived there, it wasn't considered part of the city. Now my old neighborhood is a whole new place, full of gangs. What used to be Mom's backyard is full of row houses. The outside of her fence is covered with gang graffiti. And people go in and out of the houses on Mom's street — houses where my childhood friends used to live — buying drugs and other illegal things.

In June 1971, Henry and I got married. We moved into a tiny old house in Portland that my grandfather had built decades earlier. It had a little room off the living room where my mom and my aunt slept when they were little. I'm not sure where my uncle slept, and I'm not sure how my grandparents managed to raise three children in such a tiny house. But it seemed the perfect place for Henry and me to start our life together.

Like many young couples, Henry and I drank on the weekends and went to wild parties with our friends. It didn't interfere with our work too much. Henry worked as a welder by trade and showed genius at all handy things. He could build, fix and repair anything. I mostly took office jobs when I worked, but I preferred to be a stay-at-home mom.

When I first got pregnant, I went to the same wild parties with Henry, but I didn't drink. In my sober state, I watched our friends get drunk and act foolish, and I felt embarrassed. I wanted better for our marriage. So Henry and I quit the party scene and left those friends behind. On December 1, 1972, we had our first child — Alice.

Alice looked very much like her dad: masses of black hair, dark eyes and olive skin. She was a beautiful baby. She was so beautiful that she caught the attention of another new father in the ward, and instead of taking pictures of his own child, he took pictures of our daughter.

Earlier, I mentioned drawing negative attention when going places with Henry. Well, I had issues going out in public with Alice, too — because of all the positive attention! No matter where we went, people would follow us around trying to touch her and make a fuss over her. Eventually, I just left her at home with my mom when I went off to run errands. I'm a germophobe of sorts, and I didn't like all those people touching her.

Alice's admirers couldn't tell that she had spina bifida.

The most severe form involves an opening in the spine, affecting children's ability to walk. Alice's spine wasn't completely open, but her opening was deep. Even so, Alice started walking at 9 months old. The doctors actually fussed about her condition more than we did. They wanted to perform surgery on her and told us that if they did, she'd only have a 50 percent chance of walking.

Her dad said, "This child is walking now. We're not going to put her through something that means she might not walk at all."

The doctors inserted a contraceptive coil in me after Alice's birth — the most common form of birth control back then. But when my daughter was 6 months old, I felt pregnant again, and while the doctor examined me, he removed the coil without my permission, causing a spontaneous abortion. After that horrific episode, doctors put me on a new type of contraceptive — birth control pills.

Shortly after I started the pill regimen, doctors confirmed my suspicions that I'd become pregnant again. I stopped taking the pills, and Little Henry came on May 2, 1974, with blond hair and blue eyes, just like me. Actually, he was premature. I guess the doctors were mistaken about my pregnancy while on the pill, and I really became pregnant after quitting them. Little Henry had no fingernails or toenails and did little else but sleep. Eventually, doctors diagnosed him with cerebral palsy and failure to thrive. At age 4, he weighed only 20 pounds and had limited use of his left side.

Even with my nursing background, I had much to learn about caring for a handicapped child. As small as he was, I didn't realize how easily I could harm him. I tried to give him a bath once, and after he refused to sit in the bathtub, I grabbed his little arms and set him firmly into the water.

I then realized I could have done serious harm, and I never wanted to do that again. I enrolled in a course at the children's hospital and learned to properly care for my fragile child. Our relationship grew much better after that.

Little Henry showed strokes of genius with handy things, just like his dad. My husband was so good at teaching him, desiring to push him toward greatness. One day, Henry put a sock on our tiny son's right hand, which encouraged him to hold a hammer in his weak hand. It got to where he could hammer with his left hand, and he was only a toddler. Doctors didn't expect much from Little Henry, but we learned his potential reached further than anyone could have imagined.

We tried to give our children a normal childhood in spite of their disabilities. When Little Henry was 2, we bought our first farm in Gresham, a real rundown place that we practically bought for a nickel and a dime. Definitely a fixer-upper. Before we could even move in, Henry had to replace the bathroom floor because the toilet had fallen through the floorboards. It was a project, but we were proud do-it-yourselfers. Trailer loads of garbage blanketed the backyard, and we cleared it away to reveal a beautiful hilly landscape complete with a sparkling little creek. Handy Henry took advantage of the yard's natural slopes and built a slide for the kids to ride down into the water when the weather was warm. We raised lots of animals and grew plants. Life was good.

I already told you about my passion for herbology. Like I said, doctors and modern medicine have their place, but I've learned they don't have all the answers.

Natural healing was especially important to us, given Henry's sensitivities. I call my husband a "chemical canary" because he reacts badly to chemicals. Sadly, his health problems worsened after other plastic and chemical poisonings.

Soon after our move, doctors diagnosed Henry with a connective tissue disorder that they predicted would leave him wheelchair-bound in six months. At the same time, Little Henry lost his hearing. Homeopathic remedies went a long way, but we needed something more.

My daughter Alice helped me find that something. From the moment of her birth, all my anger toward God over my grandfather's death went away. When I heard her cry for the first time, my heart melted, and I decided God must exist, and I figured he must be good to give us this beautiful, beautiful baby. As she grew older, I watched her play with my father the same way I played with the grandfather I loved so much. My father thought of her as his special little girl.

My husband, Henry, had chosen to follow Christ when he was only 9 years old. Through the window in his upstairs bedroom, he noticed a light flooding a nearby building. Once Henry discovered they offered free food in that building — a potluck — he wanted to check it out. But after he got there, he realized he didn't want to stand around in the basement eating with the other kids. Being so smart and mature for his age, he was drawn more to grownup things. He went upstairs to hear the preacher speak, and at that time, Henry sensed God ask him if he wanted to be a preacher. Henry told God no. But the preacher upstairs still moved him, and from that day forward he surrendered his life to Christ and felt his presence and protection many times.

Henry Senior trusted in the Lord years before I did, but Alice gets the credit for motivating us to go to church.

When Alice was about 5 years old, she learned about God through our babysitter, Ruth, a Christian woman who told her all about Jesus Christ's love for her. Bible stories fascinated Alice, and she really wanted to be a part of the Missionette program at Ruth's church. Soon, Ruth invited our whole family to church, and after a time, we became completely involved. Henry and I helped with the kitchen ministry and taught Sunday school. Alice joined the Missionettes. She instantly connected with people and moved them with her earnest enthusiasm. Little Henry still wasn't old enough for Royal Rangers, but he was heading there.

In 1977, I made the decision to accept Jesus Christ as my Lord and Savior. I gave my life to the Lord at a Women's Aglow meeting, shaking like a leaf as many of my church sisters watched me walk to the front and state my commitment to Jesus Christ. The experience exhilarated me, but it didn't prepare me for what came next at a women's retreat. I hadn't planned to go to the retreat at first because I smoked, and I couldn't imagine enduring an overnight trip without a cigarette.

I didn't make it through the whole retreat. After I arrived, I was prayed for, and I felt an intense healing power inside me — a precious gift from my heavenly father. I immediately determined I needed to go straight home and pray over my ailing husband and son.

Once I returned home, I laid my hands on Henry and prayed over his connective tissue disorder, channeling the Lord's healing power into his illness. Next, I placed my hands over Little Henry's ears and prayed for the Lord to restore his hearing.

Little Henry retreated to his bedroom, and out of instinct I wished him goodnight.

He turned around.

"What did you say, Mommy?"

The Lord had restored Little Henry's hearing! After witnessing this miracle, I knew without a doubt that I wanted to spend the rest of my life walking with Christ.

My prayer's affect on my husband that night was less obvious, but to this day he's never been in a wheelchair.

The kids loved playing outdoors, and as a family, we loved to go fishing. Little Henry wanted to fish all the time. In 1978, when the kids were 4 and 5, we planned a Memorial Day vacation to a campsite at Indian Lake that offered trout fishing and campfires — all the simple pleasures of outdoor life that we craved. My parents and my brother and his kids planned to meet us there, and we anticipated a great time as a family.

Two weeks before the trip, Alice woke up from her nap and shared her dream with me.

"I was on a bus with all these kids, and Jesus was our bus driver!"

"Who were these kids, Alice?" I asked.

"Oh, I don't know, Mommy. I haven't met them yet!"

A few minutes later, Little Henry woke up from his nap, and he shared the same dream with me. I don't think he'd heard his sister talking to me.

Finally it was time to head to Indian Lake for the weekend. My parents gave us a tiny round trailer house to hitch to our truck and use at the campsite. My brother was taking his own kids up, and they would be in his own camper. So I told Henry, "Why can't they ride in the canopy?" We had made the canopy much like a camper inside. I thought the kids would have more space back there, and we could keep an eye on them through the truck's rear window.

That's where we decided the kids would ride on the way to Indian Lake, with our cute miniature Collie dog to keep them company. They could sprawl out and fall asleep. Back in those days they weren't required to wear seatbelts, so we didn't have to worry about getting in trouble with the law.

As we were getting ready to go, Alice seemed a little queasy.

INSIDE OUT

"Mommy, I don't feel so good."

"What's wrong, sweetie? Do you have a headache?" Alice's spina bifida expressed itself more and more in those days. She had painful headaches and some incontinence, despite being successfully potty-trained at 9 months old.

"A little bit. I think I have the flu."

Some of her friends had the flu, but Alice didn't seem that bad, so we went ahead, anyway. It wasn't every day she had the chance to go camping with her grandparents and cousins.

We got them settled under the canopy and drove ahead, stopping in a town along the way for a bite to eat. When we checked on the kids, we saw that both of them had vomited. So we took them out and cleaned up the mess. I felt disappointed that both of them were sick, realizing the vacation would not be what we had hoped for.

When it came time to hit the road again, we wondered whether to put the kids back in the camper or to move them up with us. It was already 10 p.m. "I think they'll just sleep the rest of the way. If we move them to the cab, they'll probably fall asleep and be uncomfortable," I said, sighing.

So we put them back to bed and turned on the light in the canopy. We cracked the windows open a little to let the fresh spring air in, hoping it would curb their sickness. And then we drove on, eventually scaling the steep side of a mountain. Henry stopped and shone a light in the back of the truck to check on them. As expected, they were curled up, sound asleep with the dog.

At 1 a.m., we reached our destination at last. Henry stopped the truck and went in the back to fetch the kids, so he could tuck them to sleep in our trailer for the rest of the night.

Their bodies were both lifeless. They were just gone. I looked at the windows and noticed they were closed again.

We tried desperately to resuscitate our babies for a long time, but to no avail. The ambulance couldn't reach us up there on that mountain, so we put the kids' bodies in the car and drove down the mountain to meet the ambulance.

It was a sickening descent.

When we met the ambulance, a paramedic gave me a bit of hope.

"Your children are still alive, ma'am."

But it seemed impossible. When we reached the ER, a coroner confirmed what I already knew.

"I'm so sorry to tell you this. Your children are gone."

We learned that the kids died from carbon monoxide poisoning, the threat of which was not well known back in the '70s. When the kids vomited on our trip, I thought they were both sick with the flu. Actually, it was the first symptom of carbon monoxide poisoning.

The coroner continued, "It's good that you didn't try to revive them when you checked on them on the way up the mountain. They would have had severe brain damage at that point."

Our children died over Memorial Day weekend, and the media couldn't wait to report our story. My parents hadn't yet made it to the campsite, and they first learned of our tragedy on the car radio. "Henry Lane Jr., 4, and his 5-year-old sister Alice were found dead of apparent carbon monoxide poisoning on a Memorial Day weekend outing ..."

And that's how everyone in town found out about our loss. The family took down all the pictures of our children, trying to spare us pain. Most of our friends shied away. Nobody let me babysit their kids after my kids died.

It was like Henry and I were untouchables.

෨෨෨

"Did you kill your children on purpose?" The investigator's eyes bore into ours as he drilled Henry and me.

"Why did you put your children back there after they got sick?"

Question after question, each one accusing us of something horrible or reminding us of a terrible decision we made and couldn't fix. The police impounded our car and camper, and we never saw either again.

Ultimately, the investigators determined that by pulling the trailer, somehow that caused carbon monoxide to swirl around and go into the camper in the back of the truck.

The most perplexing part of this whole episode was

the little dog. She survived just fine. But we couldn't keep her anymore. She reminded us of losing the children, and the fact that she survived when the kids died was just too much to bear. We ended up adopting her out.

After the kids died, we never went back to the farm. We couldn't face it. So we stayed with my parents instead. Our best friends Mike and Linda lived in Coos Bay. Mike was in the Navy, and there was a Navy base there at the time — and we just needed to get away. Lost in a deep depression with no hope in sight, we thought a new environment would distract us from our inner torment. So we headed out to see them and pulled over at a beach, where we sat at a fishing dock with lots of grass and nothing else around, crying. We were just lost in darkness. Overwhelmed, we talked about driving our car over a cliff just to stop the pain.

An older man was sitting on the dock in front of us. He looked like an old fisherman, and he engaged us in conversation.

I have no idea how long he talked to us, exactly, or everything he said to us. All we knew is that we both felt better after he left. And when we turned around to thank him, he was gone — vanished. I looked out at the vast beach and field before us and wondered where he could have gone.

His message renewed our strength and helped us persevere in the years to come. We believed he was an angel.

Life stayed hard for Henry and me for a long time. We

never stopped believing in the Lord and his power, but we struggled with leading a Christian life. Health problems bogged us down. Henry had his first chemical poisoning working in a plastics factory, and I gained weight and suffered from paranoia and agoraphobia, and I drank more. I flirted with suicidal thoughts. But I loved the Lord and felt him holding on to me.

Soon, the wife of one of Henry's co-workers brought me these little pink pills called cross tops, better known as speed. I took just one of them and felt an amazing, strong rush of energy. It sped up everything in my body. I could multi-task. I could triple-task. Going from lethargy to having all this incredible energy was hard to resist. It became my drug of choice. But the thing with speed is, once you start taking it, it takes more and more pills to get the same effect.

Consequently, at the young age of 32, I had my first stroke due to drug and alcohol abuse.

೨ುೊುೊುೊು

We adopted two young blond, blue-eyed boys, ages 5 and 7, hoping to return to a normal life, but they both came from an abusive background and had many issues that we all had to face together. Henry moved us to a tiny trailer house in the national forest in La Pine, Oregon, so I could be away from people and restore my physical and mental health. After moving there, I started to grow closer to the Lord. I didn't have anything to do while the boys attended school, and Henry worked all day, so I read an entire library of the things that interested me — medicine, herbology, healing. And I also started reading my Bible more.

This time, something felt different. The words I read really spoke to my paranoid state of mind and helped to replace my confused thoughts with peace.

I felt like God showed me the perfect verses in the Bible for my situation.

"Blessed are those who mourn: for they will be comforted," I read in Matthew 5:4. I remembered how the old fisherman somehow comforted Henry and me when we grieved our children's deaths.

"Trust in the Lord with all your heart and lean not on your own understanding" (Proverbs 3:5).

And the verse that gave me hope: "Come to me, all you who are weary and burdened, and I will give you rest" (Matthew 11:28). Those words were like medicine — they helped, they healed and they gave me peace of mind. Before then, noise filled my head — no rest. Those medicinal words, when applied, gave me REST.

I listened, and with my heavenly father's help and my husband's hand and heart, I started my long walk out of my darkness and mental illness to serve my heavenly father with all my heart, mind and soul.

Henry and I were desperate to find a good church and work for the Lord. We wanted to meet other Christian friends, but more than that, we wanted to be fed spiritually. We wanted to learn more about what the Bible said and needed a good pastor and Bible study group to help illuminate God's word. Unfortunately, the mold and construction materials found in many churches aggravated Henry's chemical sensitivities. Then one day, we saw a billboard for a church that read, "Have your toolbox ready, and I will find you work." We looked at each other and concluded this was a sign from the Lord. We needed to find the right "tools" to do God's work.

We started attending Eastside Church and found they offered a class called MTI, Ministry Training Institute. I had been diagnosed with lupus by then, and Henry had been given a diagnosis of only a year to live. Pastor Dusty spoke to the person who had organized the course. After praying about it, he allowed us to study from home, like a correspondence course.

Through the course, we picked up the tools we needed to share Christ's message of forgiveness and dying on the cross to save our souls — tools like leading, gaining deeper understanding through reading the Bible and showing compassion to others. We finished and graduated and went on our first mission trip.

Around the same time, Henry became so ill from a chemical poisoning that he briefly died. He described standing against a wall with throngs of people before him, and at the front shone the glow of the heavenly father. It was then that he realized he made it to heaven, but he hadn't done that much for the Lord. So he said, "Lord, if you send me back, I'll do whatever you ask, even if it's just taking someone to church."

The Lord did send him back to earth to be with us. That's what we believe.

A little bit after that, I received a phone call.

"Hello, Lee. Do you know Abigail, a woman who attends our church?"

"I don't think so," I replied.

"She fell and broke her back several weeks ago and needs help getting to a meeting with people from church. Would you and Henry be able to drive her until she gets better?"

"Well, I'm sorry to hear about Abigail's injury," I said, confused. "We're 17 miles out of town, and this meeting is another eight miles out. I'm so sorry, but we're not able to do that."

Henry overheard the conversation and remembered what he'd promised the Lord.

"Lee, you'd better call them back and tell them we'll do it!"

When we arrived to pick up Abigail, she gave Henry a funny look and hesitated to get in our car. But eventually she warmed up to him and appreciated our help.

Henry still teetered on the brink of death, and no one at church knew except Pastor Dusty. But when we got to the church meeting, there were about 15 people there, including Abigail. A man named Samuel asked, "Henry, can we pray for you?"

Henry didn't want to discuss all his complicated medical problems, but he replied, "If you want to pray for me, pray for me."

So they anointed him with oil and started praying for him. Abigail was the first to pray.

"Heavenly Father, I pray for you to heal Henry's neck," she prayed as she laid her hands on him.

Henry wondered how Abigail knew to pray for his neck. Years before, Henry had been electrocuted, causing injury to his neck, but Abigail wouldn't have known that. Suddenly, he felt as if someone was poking him with a little cow prod. At first, he thought Abigail did it.

As the group continued praying, they touched on his different issues, and he felt a little shock each time. He was a bit perturbed that he kept getting shocked, but when he looked up and realized that no one was shocking him, he allowed them to continue praying for him.

Amazingly, his disease process stopped, and he got better and better after that.

I was still ill with several ailments, including lupus and a nerve disease called polyneuropathy that made my body go numb. I'd gone through bypass surgery and suffered from fibromyalgia. Henry would dress and bathe me, because I didn't have the energy or strength. Mostly I would just sit on the deck and read my Bible. And then I heard a voice, *I'm going to heal you.*

I thought it was just me and thought about how tired I was of being sick. I'd been sick for so long. Then, a few weeks later, I heard it again,

Lee, I'm going to heal you. And I believe it was the heavenly father because he called me by name.

So we went to Eastside Church one Sunday, and as we

were leaving, Pastor Dusty said into his microphone, "Folks, I feel like the Lord is telling us something! There's a woman here, and she's chronically ill. And if she comes forward, she will be healed!"

At once I went to the front of the church, and Pastor Dusty and a man I did not know and couldn't clearly see prayed for me. I didn't feel much different that day, but in the morning, I went out barefoot to let our little doggie out and stubbed my toe. And I cried, "Ouch!" And then I shouted, "Praise the Lord! That hurt! I felt that!"

When Henry and I first came to Eastside, we wanted a place where we could worship and be fed spiritually. And we certainly found that at Eastside Church.

When I lost my grandfather so many years ago, I didn't understand why God let that happen, and I stopped believing in him. But I was just a child then. As I matured, I learned that the Lord knows when it's time to take someone home. And someday that will be me. But my time hasn't come yet, and neither has Henry's. That's why the Lord has spared our lives many times with healing miracles beyond anything modern physicians or natural healers could imagine.

When my children passed away and went to meet Jesus and the other children on that school bus they dreamed of, Henry and I wanted to join them right away. But the Lord kept us here for many years and let us know he had a plan for us. I believe he has a unique plan for everyone. Through him, we've found so much meaning in our lives, and we've used it to serve his kingdom. We adopted two boys, saved them from abuse and raised them in a Christian home. We shared our unique story so that it might give hope and comfort to other people going through trials.

And, of course, we helped that lady get to church on Sunday.

OUT ON THE EDGE
The Story of Russ Rhoden
Written by Holly De Herrera

I draped my legs over the side of the bed, not wanting to bother my wife, who slept beside me. I sat up, slightly disoriented.

What is wrong?

I couldn't put my finger on it, but I felt lost or like I'd lost something. I just didn't know what.

Nothing had happened. No terrible dream. No fight or problems with Rhonda. I just felt *different*. Empty. Lost.

You just need to shake it off, I thought. *Grab some caffeine. Shower it away.*

But neither coffee nor a shower dislodged this feeling that settled in my bones. The day stretched on like a long, empty road ... one almost blurry to navigate. I was happy, healthy, had a great job — but something was just not right.

Sometimes people just have bad days. I spoke against the feeling, like willpower could push it back.

But days stretched into weeks, and the dreadful "feeling" hung like boulders around my neck, pressing down on my shoulders. What I didn't know was that life as I knew it wouldn't return — everything had changed. I had changed, but I had no idea why or how to find my way back.

INSIDE OUT

৵৵৵

As a boy, all I ever wanted to be was a cowboy. I imagined myself on the back of a horse, the hard saddle beneath me and an open field of cattle as far as the eye could see, sunlight shining like a fresh start all along the honey-colored horizon. But before I could ride into the sunset, my brothers and I had irrigation pipes to connect on our farm. It felt like there was mile after mile of hand line needing to be laid to water the crops. It seemed like every day all I did was lay pipes. Dad grew hay and other grains and loved life in the open air. I was just like him that way. When Dad decided I was ready, I was allowed to drive the tractor, harrow the fields and brand the cattle. The yellow wheat heads waving in the cool morning air, row after row of them, orderly and disappearing into the distance — that was my place. I felt like me there. Like I was who I was supposed to be somehow.

But life has a way of changing on you, and high school brought new challenges. Wrestling was my thing, and I loved the thrill of carving out my own name in a different way. I had no idea, though, that my junior year I would meet a girl, we would get married and less than a year later my beautiful baby girl Rita would be born. I didn't realize that I'd be divorced only a year later. Life had a way of changing from one thing to another so quickly.

It wasn't hard for me to get into partying. So many of my friends did it, and I became known as the life of the party. It felt natural and exhilarating to belong.

"Russ!" My friends would crowd in, all smiles and happiness, even though they were blurry around the edges and off kilter. Music was throbbing in the background, and girls were always around, reminding me that I was alive and wanted and could still feel something, regardless of how shallow it went.

It didn't touch me deep inside. But the person everyone saw and the person I wanted them to see was happy and didn't have a care in the world.

I knew things had gotten out of hand, but there were times my life was being lived without me even knowing how it was happening. A tidal wave passed through, and who was I to stop it? This was the person I had become, the person everyone expected me to be. It felt like a trap and liberty at the same time. I'm not sure why I chose what I knew would leave me feeling like an empty feed sack, but I did. Over and over and over.

Partying became a way of life, not for the partying itself but for the camaraderie of my friends. It became a comfortable rhythm, one I could count on delivering what it promised. Work hard all week, but on the weekend, live it up. There weren't a lot of entertainment options in a small town — go to parties, meet girls, laugh with friends. The weekends were just an occasion to get together and drink beer and use drugs. However, partying became more than a weekend event and eventually spilled over into everyday life. I pretended life had purpose and that happiness was as simple as a feeling. As simple as a short-lived high.

INSIDE OUT

"Want to go lift some weights?" my brother Mark asked me. He'd found a gym he wanted me to try.

I patted my belly and answered, "Sure, why not. May help with the partying skills." We made plans to meet up at the place Mark discovered to lift.

I got out of my car in front of an old two-story house that had been converted into a gym. I headed inside and was immediately assaulted by the smell of sweaty men, strong enough to deter any women within a five-mile radius. But despite that fact, there was a different feel to the place. Something comfortable, familiar and, strange to say, peaceful.

All around the room stood different kinds of weights. And scrawled across the gray-white walls were words, Bible verses I figured out, with markers in piles so you could add to the graffiti.

"Hi, I'm Darwin Grimm. Welcome." Then he grinned like he had been expecting and finally reuniting with a long-lost friend.

I shook his hand, then he turned to my brother Mark and stuck out his hand. "Welcome back, brother."

Mark tilted his head toward me. "My brother Russ."

Darwin chuckled. "Well, you've come to the right place. Here we like to say that it's not just about the physical. It's also about the mental and spiritual. You need all three to be in line. To be healthy and whole."

I knew as soon as he said it that I had been found out. He wasn't fooled by my normal appearance, my "have it all together" way. Somehow Grimm seemed to see past that, into the darkness, and I felt both defensive and relieved.

"So here's the deal," Grimm said. "If you try it out and want to come back, we don't ask for much. Membership is just a few dollars a month, but we ask that you come to the church next door at least once a month, too." He patted my shoulder like he could see me squirming. "If you can do these things, we'd love to have you."

"So, what do you think?" my brother asked me. "Wanna join?"

I managed to mumble, "Sure thing." But even though it seemed like an easy arrangement, I wasn't sure at all. The stakes were higher than they appeared at first. Many things in my life were a mess, even if it seemed the whole world thought otherwise. *What could possibly be wrong with Russ? He has it all!* Only they were wrong. I felt like I was drowning.

But Mark and I did start going to the gym regularly. I craved those times. I felt free from expectations. Free from needing to be the life of the party. I could just go work out. I could just be. And the other people there had something different about them that made me want to be around them. People were there as much for the atmosphere as for the weights.

We still needed to meet our monthly quota of attending the church next door, and so we went.

Sitting down at that church was like being hit in the side of the head with a board. I had agreed to go, assuming it wouldn't do anything. Wouldn't mean anything. How could it? I wasn't about to give up my life, the way I lived, and I was sure that wouldn't fly with God. So I sat down on the cushioned pew at the church, several rows back on the aisle.

Aside from being in church for Sunday school as a small boy and for a handful of funerals and weddings since then, I just didn't attend. The whole thing felt foreign. I leaned back, wondering when it would be over with and thinking about my plans for the rest of the weekend. That's when Grimm started speaking.

He talked about freedom and purpose, and he explained that the only place to find it was through Jesus, and it felt like the man was talking straight to me and showing me that something was missing in my life. He invited anyone who wanted to give his or her life over to the Lord to come to the front.

Somehow I ended up moving down the long line of people seated in our row, my brother with me, and heading toward the front. It was like I was watching some other guy. *Why was I standing and walking? Wasn't I too far out to be saved?* Still, somehow, I believed that God saw just where I was and knew what he was getting — like he didn't miss a thing but still wanted me.

Jesus, the son of God, the one who spent time with the kind of people nobody else thought worthy of more than a passing thought, who carried a cross on his back, who'd been nailed on it, hands and feet nailed tight, who could have said, "No," and used his power to fight back — he'd done all of it for me. Me.

Gratefulness spread through me, filling up the empty spaces, flooding the chambers and rooms inside. I looked over, and my brother was right there with me, tears in his eyes.

They played a worship song. The words wove into my thoughts. "I love you, Lord, and I lift my voice to worship you ... take joy, my king, in what you hear. May it be a sweet, sweet sound in your ear."

I wanted my life to count for something. I wanted to be a sweet sound to Jesus. I wanted the strength to live out a new life. A new joy and peace overwhelmed me. But even though everything inside me felt changed, when it was all over, I realized I'd be going home to my same roommates. They'd be drinking, and I would join them as if I was the same person who left there earlier that day. I had my friends who knew me for the fun-loving guy who was always up for a good time. Only I felt different.

My experience with God had been as real as any high, only it had gone so deep, I knew I was different. Still, not different enough to make me brave enough to change. I knew before I even stepped in to my place that this "new me" wouldn't fly. And so I wouldn't tell people, and I wouldn't give them reason to change their opinion of me.

I would be like Peter from the Bible when he denied he even knew his best friend, Jesus, because of his own fear and shame. I would deny the God who saved my soul, who I'd promised to follow only hours before. I knew it before I even saw their faces or expectant grins.

And so I lived a double life: going to church and

attending foundations of faith classes with Reverend Grimm, my brother and also my mom, then heading out to live my party life.

Into my double world stepped Rhonda. It was the typical Friday night of partying, and even though I was high, I could see she was beautiful, with big brown eyes. She saw something in me that I am sure didn't exist, but still our relationship began, first just for fun, just whenever we happened to show up at the same get-together. And later it intensified, and I knew sober or not that she and I were meant to be together. Regardless of the ups and downs we faced, somehow we both still knew that. Rhonda decided to move to Reno. She had family there and wanted a chance at something new. So she left to go work at a casino, and I followed her there.

I left Prineville thinking it would be nice to start over. Only starting over looked an awful lot like the same thing in a different place. In Reno, I didn't attend church anymore. My last connections to that life seemed to pull away from me. Some nights I woke up sobbing, right out of my sleep. I was wounded so deep inside and felt so weak. I wanted to live for God, but I didn't have the strength to push back against the pressure to fit in. I felt like a hypocrite, like such a stinking liar that I couldn't stand to be in my own skin. I wanted to live for the Lord, but I just didn't have the strength to do it.

I had God's spirit living inside me, like being deeply in love and knowing without any doubt that I was loved back, only I never was strong enough to tell anyone, and I was too much of a weakling to change anything, to actually show how different I was inside.

Rhonda and I got married, the best day of my life. I loved her so much and loved that I got to be with her forever. We decided we'd had enough of Reno and came home to start our family. Our baby girl Jessica was born. Her birth gave me a sense of responsibility, and I started working for a local mill. I worked the graveyard shift, then slept just a couple hours before heading out to work on my uncle's ranch. There, my father-in-law, Jim, and I spent long sweltering days in the sun together, each on our horse, gathering cattle to be worked and then moved to another pasture.

Rhonda's dad, Jim, became a best friend. One who didn't expect something that stole away my self-respect but who just let me be. It felt so good to have that. I longed to be me and to be known without trying so hard. I loved my friends, and I considered myself lucky to be surrounded by a town of people whom I knew and who knew me.

I eventually changed jobs and started working in the woods, working the landing, skidding logs and then becoming a timber faller. I loved the smell and freedom of being in the woods. It was hard work and satisfying. About this time, Rhonda and I had our second daughter, Jade.

Sitting at the bar after work each day, grit and the sap of trees on my hands, I would nurse a beer, letting the sharp edges inside me soften.

INSIDE OUT

"So the wife doesn't mind you hanging with us every day?"

"Nah, she's fine with it." I saw my wife's big brown eyes watching me as if she sat across the room at a table. Was she really okay with this, with me? Or did she just keep her truth hidden like I did?

Not long after our second little girl came along, Rhonda and I agreed the partying had to slow down. We didn't want our kids to grow up in a home where alcohol was commonplace. Where their dad spent more time out with friends than at home tucking them into bed at night. So we gradually phased partying out of our lives. I gave up heavy drinking and the other substances I had been using. Cold turkey. It was like I was the one who had held on to the substances, instead of the other way around.

I started working for the irrigation district, in a way reliving my childhood days of laying irrigation pipe on our farm. Only this was different. I was grown and making decent money and living the American dream with a nice house and cars and looking to all the world like I had it all. Beautiful wife, beautiful kids, decent job. But one morning, I woke up aware of the smudged dark spot that seemed to live in my chest. I thought I could shake it — I was just feeling a little down, but one day led to the next and then a week into a month, and it eventually grew to a gaping cavern, and fear took up residence in that space so dark and strong I felt I might scream. That's when the panic attacks started.

First was the sense of loss, of emptiness. Then small

attacks began. Then panic attacks so overpowering I thought they'd kill me. I started planning our outings based on ease of escape. Sitting in the middle of a row of people wasn't an option. I needed easy access to a nearby door. Bathrooms became my hiding place, and it was always better if they were single stalls, rather than a whole row of urinals and stalls. I didn't want anyone to hear me crying.

The attacks became more and more frequent, leaving me fearful every minute of every day. But even though I wanted the terror to stop, I knew doctors and pills couldn't do anything for me. I knew this was something inside that drugs wouldn't quell. I knew that would be like trying to use a dam to block out the ocean.

All I had to hold onto was a Bible verse I'd learned: "No, in all these things we are more than conquerors through him who loved us" (Romans 8:37).

I spoke those words I remembered from my church days, hoping to gain control. Only, again, I wasn't able to. I was full of fear, and instead of doing battle, I cowered and hid, waiting for the darkness to pass so I could stand up straight again and pretend not to be losing it.

But pretending didn't work for long. When Jim was diagnosed with lung cancer, I could hardly process it. Jim was the quiet cowboy type, and one day I stepped into his garage knowing we needed to have a man-to-man talk.

"Jim, you know I love you too much to lie to you." I paused. *What was I saying? I'd been lying to everyone for years and hiding my love for God.* I shook my head and started again. "Well, I need to tell you the truth now. You know there's a heaven to gain. There's a creator who created all this. We don't have to miss out on heaven. I have that hope inside me, even though I haven't been living it. Still, I know it's true."

So I shared with Jim about Jesus and how it wasn't too late. That Jesus loved him, died for him and was waiting patiently, with open arms. Jim would belong to him if he'd only just ask and believe. He only nodded, always the quiet type. But on his deathbed, sometime later, he did receive the hope of heaven when a local pastor talked to him about the same thing. When he let go and finally took his last breath, I believe he did so with peace, like clean air in blackened lungs, unable to really soak it all in but trusting he would experience God's fullness soon enough.

Still, walking out of his house and out to my truck, I couldn't help but ask myself what made me such an expert anyhow. Who was I to talk about the God I had been too ashamed to even mention to my friends? Who I had shoved way back into a spare room I only visited when someone was dying? I built that space and walled God in away from the rest of me, from the rest of my life. Still, I couldn't help but be a little proud of doing the right thing by Jim when it came right down to it. That was a big step for me.

One day an attack came on again, and I crawled, face to the ground, crying and screaming in the quiet of my home, thankful that my wife, who saw me as a pillar of strength, was out. It was like hissing snakes moving around me, under my chin. Pulsing fear made me feel like I had lost it. "I want to die, God! Do you hear me?" My screams echoed in my muted living room. "I can't do this anymore!" Somehow I managed to crawl to my room and stand up to reach for my Bible, untouched for so many years and coated with dust. I rubbed my shaking hand over the cover, and it seemed like an old friend who had waited patiently for me to remember. Stumbling to the kitchen, I opened it and sat down, the crinkle of the parchment-thin pages hushing, hushing. Again I spoke to the quiet, "I don't know what I'm doing or if I'll even understand this, God. But if you'll save me from this, I will read this every day of my life."

Sobs overtook me, and I lay my head on the pages, and they cooled the fire just a little, like a mom's gentle hand stroking her boy's damp hair away from a feverish brow.

The attacks didn't disappear. There were still days I'd be out of commission, crying out to the Lord, begging him to dull the fears, to drag me away from the ledge I felt near falling over. I would beg God, "Pull me back just one inch! God, I know I did it before. I turned my back on you, but I promise never again. I'll die before I ever turn my back on you!" And I believe he heard me and lay beside me on the floor on my worst days, when I felt sure I wasn't going to make it, and he calmed me, reminding me that I wasn't walking this out alone. He was lifting my hands up above my head, telling me I was a victor despite how I felt, all because he had my back. He had gone through the worst thing possible himself on that cross.

INSIDE OUT

I attended Grimm's church now and then. I sat in the back hoping to soak up something good, something to help me get things straight. Somehow my life remained a constant contradiction.

During a community service on Easter week, Dusty, the pastor from Eastside Church who had come to preach as a guest at a local church, came right over to me after the service and said, "I'd like to pray for you."

I turned to the side, thinking maybe he was talking to the person on my left, only nobody was there. "Me?" I pointed to my chest, feeling heat creep into my face, down my neck. *He knows I'm a fake!*

"If you don't mind." He sat down beside me, putting his big hand on my shoulder. I felt myself sink a little in the seat. Then he said, "Lord, I believe you told me this young man would someday preach your word. I believe you have plans for his life. I pray a blessing on him that he would not hide from you, from your calling." And just like that, he was done. He squeezed my arm and moved on.

I sat there for a while, heart pumping like a hot fist and eyes searching the back of the pew in front of me. *Preach? Me?* Nothing felt further from the truth. I was a coward and hadn't told anyone but Jim about God, or about me for that matter. No, the man must be deluded or just hoping to inspire something that didn't exist into being true. My mind went back to a day when one of my friends heard I was going to church.

"You're not going to be one of those 'Jesus freaks,' are you?"

"Of course not!" I said.

One day, my dad called on the phone. "Russ, I need you to come by the house."

"Why? What's going on?"

"Just come by, okay?"

Dad wasn't one to waste words, but still his abbreviated call unnerved me. I got into my car and pressed the gas as much as I could without risking a speeding ticket. A few minutes later, I arrived at my parents' house. We sat together in the kitchen. I settled in and took a slow, deep breath. A burning in my chest started, and I prayed quietly that God would hold all my junk back this time so I could just listen and hear what my dad needed to say. *In all these things ...* A new smell I'd never noticed at their house hung in the room. It was a sickening smell that I'd only experienced once before. When my father-in-law had cancer.

"Russ, we just went to the doctor's office," my dad said. "I have spots on my lungs, tumors. They say it looks like cancer. There will be tests to confirm that but ..."

There. He said it. *God!* I prayed. *I can't handle it if he dies. Don't take my dad. Don't take my dad! Please, I need more time with him. Please give me more time!*

My dad never went to church with Mom, so I had no clue what he believed. Did he have any hope beyond this life?

Before I left that day, I simply said, "I'll be praying, Dad. I love you." There was so much more I wanted to say, but nothing would come.

He blinked against tears and nodded curtly. "Thank you."

Waiting for the results of the biopsy seemed to take years. During the long week, I prayed almost without ceasing, on the floor on my face, while at work, with Rhonda, in the bathroom. All the prayers blurred, a constant vigil.

The phone rang shrill against the quiet of the house. It rang again. I knew the results were due back that day. *Ring!* I didn't know if I could pick it up. If I could be strong and listen when my dad said he was going to die. *Ring!*

"Hello?" I said the word like I was flinching, waiting to be decked.

"Russ?"

"Dad?" We both knew who the other was, but we seemed stuck on trying to delay. I could hear a quiet sob on the other end of the line. "Dad? What's wrong? Did you hear back?" I was a little boy again, and the irrigation pipes went on for miles and miles, and all I wanted to do was jump on a horse and ride off away from it, out into the wide, wide open where nothing could hurt me and I didn't have to be anything but me and I didn't need to say anything to comfort my dying dad, because how can I do that? How can I possibly do that?

"Russ." He gulped in, and I could hear him swallowing. Sniffing back the tears. "Russ, God answered your prayers. Your mother's prayers." His last words came out in a sob. "I don't have any cancer!"

What? How could that be? Lung spots, big dark ones like he'd described a week before didn't just go from malignant to benign. No, that didn't just happen. *Was I just hearing what I wanted? Was any of this happening? Was I finally crazy, living in my pretend world alone, talking to the wall?*

"Did you hear? He answered!" I knew in that moment that it was real. And my very real Jesus had healed my father.

గొ గొ గొ

I was out working for the irrigation district one day, sitting inside the cab of my backhoe. All the other guys I worked with had gone into town to get a part. And it was like God himself set up a divine appointment with me. In the cab of that machine, I sat with my headphones on, music playing in my head, working. The world muted, and I felt like I could relax. I was alone and didn't have anyone to worry about. Everything seemed to move in slow motion, the movement of the rig, the tumble of soil in front of me. Then something happened that nearly knocked me from my metal seat.

I heard, audibly, a voice saying, *Take those headphones off. I have something to tell you.*

I wobbled a bit, turned around, looked over one shoulder, then turned again and looked over the other. There was nothing in the cab with me except this tangible peace, as if the small space had filled with the smell of the prairie, the wind tipping off the trees and no sense of panic at all. I turned straight then and kept working when I heard it again.

Take those headphones off. I have something to tell you.

Again I jerked. *What was this? Some kind of joke? Had I officially fallen off my rocker?* But, no, there wasn't a person for miles around, and I didn't have that crazy, heart-pained feeling I had grown so accustomed to.

I reached up and pulled the headphones off, then turned off the backhoe so that only silence filled the air around me.

"All right. I'm listening." Maybe I was crazy. Crazy people don't realize they are, though, right?

I want you to preach my word.

"What? How?" I could feel such a calm, even given the words I'd just heard. It made no sense. How could I preach anything to anyone? I couldn't even handle answering questions in my Bible study. "Do I quit my job? Go to school? What?"

Again the answer came so calm and assured. *No, stay where you are. This is where I want to use you now.*

Tears fell unchecked down my face. Hadn't Pastor Dusty said as much years and years before? Somehow God wanted to use me for something big, despite my total inadequacy. Despite the fact that only in the last few years could I stand to tell anyone I even knew him! How could it be possible that the God of the universe saw anything he could use in me? Afterward I thought it was like Moses and the burning bush. A holy God talking to a man who stuttered, asking him to help lead the Israelites out of captivity. I figured, *God really is in the business of employing losers.*

I don't know how long I sat there crying. My insides felt like they were being transformed. Like purpose lodged itself in the empty, dark place where I hid all my fears and shame.

I continued living as best I could with my issues. I attended church where I'd met Jesus years before and coped with my anxiety, feeling more and more settled. But then the pastor preached a sermon about getting out of my comfort zone, and somehow I knew I was just hiding out, like a recluse who moved further and further away from people and life.

I felt deep inside that it was time for me to move to a new church, not because they failed or there was anything wrong with where I was, but because I needed to force myself out of my rut. It was as if God was showing me that I needed to quit trying to be comfortable. *But,* I argued against the idea, *my friends go to this church. My mom!* Still, the feeling pressed on me, gently pushing me to make the change.

So I began attending Eastside Church on Wednesday nights. I could feel myself growing in my understanding of God and his good plans for my life. I knew the life I was living wasn't really living at all. I was in a perpetual bracing against what would come. I had come so far from the outgoing, life-of-the-party guy I once was. Though I didn't miss the party life, I missed feeling or at least appearing confident.

One day Rhonda and I were driving down the road when I decided she should know what had been going on, especially since I seemed to be having one of the heart-attack moments I knew too well, only this was more painful and wouldn't go away.

"I don't know how to tell you this …" I looked quickly over my shoulder at her, then flicked my eyes back to the road.

Rhonda turned in her seat and gave me her full attention.

I pulled in a breath, in through my nose, slowly out through my mouth. Somehow I managed to begin and then told her everything. About the fear and panic attacks. About me hiding it and lying about all those times I needed to go home for this or that. About never letting her fully see my heart, even from the start of our marriage. About hiding my experience with God. About thinking I was going crazy. She just listened as I poured it all out.

"Even now," I said, "it feels like 10,000 needles are poking into my arm." She moved her hand up and down my arm, down to my fingers that were clutching the steering wheel, then back up again, massaging. But the sensation didn't go away.

"I'm taking you to the hospital!" she insisted.

"No," I said. "I will be fine; it will pass."

But by the time we arrived back home, I felt as though an elephant sat on my chest. I walked back to my room, sat on the edge of the bed trying to calm my heart rate. *This was all in my head, right?* But I couldn't get past the horrible pressure.

I ran out to Rhonda, the sensation so strong I couldn't say anything. My mouth was open, but no words came out. It was the worst attack I'd ever had.

I could only hope she'd understand. She looked at me, her eyebrows raised, and simply snatched her purse off the counter and said, "Get in the car. We're going to the ER."

Any other time I would have refused, certain that what ailed me came from somewhere in my heart that no doctor could touch. I didn't have anything against medicine — I was just stubborn, and I wanted to demand to God, "If you are who you say you are, heal me!" But this time, I was scared. I considered that I might be dying, and even though I had begged God so many times to kill me rather than living this way one more day, I realized that I didn't want my life to count for nothing. How could I leave my girls, my wife, my family without having added anything to this world? No, I had things I needed to do. In my mind, I screamed at God, *If you are who you say you are, heal me!*

Hours later, sitting on the hospital table, the paper sheet sticking to the backs of my legs, I was informed that there was absolutely nothing wrong with my heart. Nothing that showed up on the scans or blood work to explain why my chest hurt, why my arm went numb.

"You're healthy as far as I can tell. You're possibly having anxiety and panic attacks." The doctor delivered the news with little sympathy. "Maybe some rest and drink plenty of water."

I chuckled. Yeah, I was healthy. I felt like an idiot sitting there, wearing nothing but a hospital robe so thin and revealing. The doctor added, "Anxiety can make us feel all kinds of things that aren't there. Have you been under a lot of pressure lately?"

What could I say? *This has been going on for seven years?* I swallowed my humiliation and mumbled something about being busy. He nodded like that solved everything and signed off on the sheet of paper. "I can write a script for a drug that can calm anxiety."

"No. Thank you. I'll be fine."

With a nod he left.

છ્છ્છ્

The panic attacks continued. I walked with a limp and sometimes felt I couldn't make it another day, another hour, another minute. It worsened when the irrigation company asked me to become a manager. My first instinct was to say, "Of course not! I can't lead a group of people. I can't even handle speaking up in Sunday school!" But Pastor Dusty encouraged me to take the job. I argued, "They've obviously got the wrong guy! I'm a timber faller. I operate machinery. That's what I do." But he persisted and encouraged me to think it through before turning the job down outright. And somehow I did. I said yes because I knew hiding wasn't helping. I needed to pretend I was brave until maybe I believed it myself.

That job brought a barrage of planning meetings, budget meetings and staff meetings, and I was the guy they wanted to lead them. What were they thinking? Little by little, I did it. Somehow. *We are more than conquerors ...* And I managed to convince them — and myself, a little bit — that I could do it well. It helped to do the job with my Biblical principals in mind. I was determined to be honest, have integrity, care for the staff and never compromise what was right for what might make more money. I truly felt myself becoming a leader. And every week at church, I would go forward for prayer. I desperately wanted to be totally free. To have all of my life match up.

My begging for more time with Dad had come to pass. Several years of getting to enjoy time with him were like a priceless gift to me. I wanted to soak up as much of his strength as possible. But the day came when I stood beside my father's deathbed. Though he had seen the miracle of his own healing, my dad shared with me that he never actually told God that he was his.

His eyes looked so helpless, I conjured courage to speak. "I know I haven't really shared a lot about the more private things in life, like my faith. But now's not the time for me to chicken out. Dad, I think you know that I have the spirit of God living in me, like Mom, and I don't want you to die without having it in you, too."

He shook his head so slightly, I almost missed it. He flinched as he spoke. "I'd feel like a cheater waiting until now, after a whole life ... after he healed me the first time."

"That doesn't matter, though, don't you see?" I told him about how Jesus had invited the guy hanging beside him on the cross to join him in heaven that very day after living who-knows-what kind of terrible life. I described Matthew 20 with him as well, the parable of the workers in the vineyard and how the Lord invites us all in to his kingdom, and some of us don't respond until late in life.

"Dad," I said, "you may have missed out on the blessing of serving God in this life, but you don't have to miss out on heaven."

Dad seemed to understand. He decided to quit trying to brave it out on his own and give his life, the little left of it, to Jesus. I didn't have much time left with him on earth, but I trusted I would see him again someday. Believing that didn't stop the horrible pain, so deep and so real I had trouble not stumbling with its weight. And a small part of me envied him. He'd found peace. He was with God, free from the constant mess I tried so hard to run from.

One Wednesday night, Dusty was preaching on getting fully in the boat. Not living two lives but fully committing to what you've chosen. I imagined myself with one foot in the boat and the other on the dock and the boat moving and my leg pressing down so hard on the planks of the dock that the boards were flying up into the air. *Get in the boat! All the way in!*

When Dusty invited people to come forward for prayer, I practically ran forward. Soon a group of men surrounded me, hands pressed on my shoulders, praying. I prayed quietly, "Lord, I'm ready. I'm all in! I give you all of it! All my fears and reservations." Then something broke in me, like a dam holding back blessings, and I felt peace inside for the first time since that day I first came to Jesus.

Healed! Instantly healed. After that, I didn't have a single anxiety or panic attack, and I felt a quiet assurance that it was over for good.

After seven years of living hell, it was over. I was healed that night. It was as if Jesus himself took that burden and carried it away for me. It was nothing I did, except for maybe my willingness to be all in with God and to quit hiding away. I felt transformed and alive and free. Those were the hardest years of my life, but you know, I wouldn't trade that time because it's what drove me to that closet to dust off the Bible.

"No, in all these things we are more than conquerors through him who loved us. For I am convinced that neither death nor life, neither angels nor demons, neither the present nor the future, nor any powers; neither height nor depth nor anything else in all creation, will be able to separate us from the love of God that is in Christ Jesus our Lord" (Romans 8:37-39).

I felt so thankful to so many who helped me and continued to help me walk this journey — my family, especially my mom, who I know prayed for me all those years and held firm to her faith in the Lord; my amazing wife and daughters, always my greatest encouragers; brother Mark for the invitation that changed my life; Reverend Grimm for showing me who Jesus is; Pastor Dusty for his friendship and discipleship; my church family, whom I could always count on; and my friends and community I loved.

Since that day, the Lord and Eastside Church have given me a lot of opportunities. Things I couldn't have imagined possible before. Things I could never have done without the door Christ opened for me. With the Lord's help, I have run marathons and spoken to hundreds. I've trained missionaries and led mission teams, helping send them out all over the world, sharing about the healing hand of God. I've preached and officiated at marriages, sometimes even funerals, sharing my faith with those old friends from whom I once hid it. And even better, my wife joined with me in this. The field of the future opened wide for me, larger than the one of my childhood dreams, and I've been riding into it without fear of what will come. I'm out in the open with the wind and the sun warm on my face, on my hands. I became who God always planned for me to be. I became whole and completely his. In the center of his plan and far, far from that terrible edge I came to know too well. I became free.

"For I am not ashamed of the gospel of Christ, for it is the power of God to salvation for everyone who believes ..." (Romans 1:16)

"... but with God all things are possible." (Matthew 19:26)

CONCLUSION

My heart is full. When I became a pastor, my desire was to change the world. My hope was to see people encouraged and the hurting filled with hope. As I read this book, I saw that passion being fulfilled. However, at Eastside Church, rather than being content with our past victories, we are spurred to believe that many more can occur.

Every time we see another changed life, it increases our awareness that God really loves people and he is actively seeking to change lives. Think about it: How did you get this book? We believe you read this book because God brought it to you seeking to reveal his love to you. Whether you're a man or a woman, blue collar or no collar, a parent or a student, we believe God came to save you. He came to save all of us from the hellish pain we've wallowed in and to offer real joy and the opportunity to share in real life that will last forever through faith in Jesus Christ.

Do you have honest questions that such radical change is possible? It seems too good to be true, doesn't it? Each of us at Eastside Church warmly invites you to come and check out our church family. Freely ask questions, examine our statements, see if we're "for real" and, if you choose, journey with us at whatever pace you are comfortable. You will find that we are far from perfect.

Our scars and sometimes open wounds are still healing, but we just want you to know God is still completing the process of authentic life change in us. We still make mistakes in our journey, like everyone will. Therefore, we acknowledge our continued need for each other's forgiveness and support. We need the love of God just as much as we did the day before we believed in him.

If you are unable to be with us, yet you intuitively sense you would really like to experience such a life change, here are some basic thoughts to consider. If you choose, at the end of this conclusion, you can pray the suggested prayer. If your prayer genuinely comes from your heart, we believe you will experience the beginning stages of authentic life change, similar to those you have read about.

How does this change occur?

Recognize that what you're doing isn't working. Accept the fact that Jesus desires to forgive you for your bad decisions and selfish motives. Realize that without this forgiveness, you will continue a life separated from God and his amazing love. In the Bible, the book of Romans, chapter 6, verse 23 tells us that the result of sin (seeking our way rather than God's way) is death, but the gift that God freely gives is everlasting life found in Jesus Christ.

Believe in your heart that God passionately loves you and wants to give you a new heart. Ezekiel 11:19 reads, "I will give them singleness of heart and put a new spirit

CONCLUSION

within them. I will take away their stony, stubborn heart and give them a tender, responsive heart" (NLT).

Believe in your heart that "if you confess with your mouth that Jesus is Lord and believe in your heart that God raised him from the dead, you will be saved" (Romans 10:9 NLT).

Believe in your heart that because Jesus paid for your failure and wrong motives, and because you asked him to forgive you, he has filled your new heart with his life in such a way that he transforms you from the inside out. Second Corinthians 5:17 reads, "When someone becomes a Christian, he becomes a brand new person inside. He is not the same anymore. A new life has begun!"

Why not pray now?

Lord Jesus, if I've learned one thing in my journey, it's that you are God and I am not. My choices have not resulted in the happiness I hoped they would bring. Not only have I experienced pain, I've also caused it. I know I am separated from you, but I want that to change. I am sorry for the choices I've made that have hurt myself and others and denied you. I believe your death paid for my sins, and you are now alive to change me from the inside out. Would you please do that now? I ask you to come and live in me so that I can sense you are here with me. Thank you for hearing and changing me. Now please help me know when you are talking to me, so I can cooperate with your efforts to change me. Amen.

Prineville's unfolding story of God's love is still being written — and your name is in it. I hope to see you this Sunday!

Pastor Dusty Flegel
Eastside Church
Prineville, Oregon

We would love for you to join us at Eastside Church!

Our service times are:
Sunday mornings - 9:30 a.m.
Wednesday nights - 6:45 p.m.

We are located at:
3174 NE 3rd Street, Prineville, OR 97754

To learn more about us or our full range of children's, youth and adult ministries, check out our Web site at www.eastsidefoursquare.org

Call us at 541.447.3791

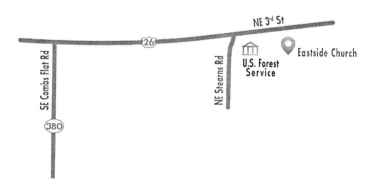